Classic
RICE DISHES

Over 100 recipes from around the world

EDITED BY JANET SWARBRICK

APPLE

Introduction

o   o   o

*R*ice is one of the oldest foods known to man and forms the staple diet for well over half the human race. It is therefore undeniably the world's most important food. There are around 40,000 different varieties of rice grains and it is not surprisingly one of the most versatile of the cereal crops.

Rice was cultivated in China as far back as 5,000 BC and may originally have been found wild in the foothills of the Himalayas. It took many centuries and the development of trade routes from the Far East to bring rice to Europe, where it first emerged as a popular and widely known food around the 17th century. Now internationally popular, rice features in the cooking of Spain, Italy, Portugal and South America as well as the oriental countries. Rice is an essential buffer food with many Chinese, Indian and oriental dishes.

As it requires no preparation and is so easily stored in the home, rice is the ideal food for busy cooks. There is no wastage – any leftover rice quickly becomes the base for a rice/vegetable dish, a rice salad, or with additions, a savoury meal. Many people cook double quantities for just this reason.

Rice is easy to digest and the processed form which does not require washing, if cooked with the minimum liquid, retains most of the nutrients. For those who are still more health conscious, brown rice (see page 8) is the most nutritious of all.

Mastering the art of cooking rice well is straightforward if you follow instructions on packets and in recipes. Timing is crucial with rice cookery. It is advisable to follow instructions carefully for the first few times that you cook rice and to watch it carefully while it is cooking.

Rice is good to eat. It has at last lost its image of a super-starchy food and can be sensibly included in calorie controlled diets. It is a source of quick energy, it contains some protein and the important B vitamins and as the perfect foil for so many fish, meat and vegetable dishes, it really deserves to be part of your weekly menu.

MAIN TYPES OF RICE

Rice is one of the easiest foods to cook, and yet many people find themselves with a glutinous mess at the end of the cooking time. This may have something to do with the many varieties available and the confusion arising over the specially processed types which are now on sale. It is advisable to read the packet when buying rice to ensure that you have selected the correct grain for your purpose.

The main types of rice are: long-grain (Patna) rice; long-grain brown rice; basmati rice (all long-grain rice); Italian risotto rice; "Carolina" or short-grain rice (both short-grain rice); ground rice; rice flour; rice flakes; wild rice.

Fidellos Tostados

○ ○ ○

Spanish Sephardic Jews have been eating a very thin vermicelli-like pasta called fidellos for centuries. It is also popular in Greece, introduced by Spanish Jews when they fled Spain during the Inquisition. Cooks often break the pasta coils and throw in rice as in this recipe.

SERVES 6

350g/12oz package
   vermicelli or angel
   hair pasta in coils
100g/3½oz American
   long-grain rice
60ml/2 tbsp olive oil
200g/7oz can tomatoes,
   drained

450–750ml/¾–1¼pt
   chicken stock or water
5ml/1 tsp salt
2.5ml/½ tsp dried
   oregano
freshly ground black
   pepper
fresh coriander leaves

○ In a dry large, heavy-bottomed frying pan, over medium–high heat, heat pasta and rice until golden brown, stirring frequently, 5–7 minutes. (It does not matter if pasta breaks a little.)

○ Add olive oil, tomatoes, chicken stock or water, salt, oregano and black pepper to taste. Bring to a boil; reduce heat to medium and simmer, stirring often to unwind pasta, 7–10 minutes. Reduce heat to low, cover and cook 10 minutes longer until all the liquid is absorbed and pasta and rice are tender. Turn into a serving bowl and garnish with coriander leaves.

Curried Almond Rice

○ ○ ○

Cubans adore peas and rice. The Curry Butter Log in this recipe can be made in advance to complement rice dishes, prawns or chicken, plain hot vegetables and grilled tomatoes.

SERVES 4

15ml/1 tbsp Curry
   Butter Log softened
750ml/1¼pt water
275g/10oz rice

125/4oz frozen green
   peas, thawed and
   cooked (optional)
30ml/2 tbsp sliced
   almonds, toasted, if
   desired

CURRY BUTTER LOG

1 medium onion, minced
225g/8oz butter,
   softened and divided
   in half
30ml/2 tbsp curry
   powder

60ml/4 tbsp prepared
   chutney, minced
2.5ml/½ tsp freshly
   ground white pepper

○ Make the Curry Butter Log first. In a small saucepan over moderately low heat, cook onion in half of the butter, stirring until softened. Stir in the curry powder, chutney and white pepper. Let mixture cool.

○ In a bowl, cream together remaining butter and the curry mixture.

○ Reserve 15ml/1 tbsp of the mixture and transfer the rest of the mixture in the shape of a 30cm/12in log onto a piece of freezer paper or plastic wrap and roll up, twisting the ends of the paper like a party popper to seal. Refrigerate until firm or freeze. Each yields about a dozen 1 tsp pats.

○ In a 20cm/8in frying pan, melt the reserved Curry Butter. Stir in water. Cover and heat to boiling. Stir in rice, reduce heat, cover and simmer about 12 minutes, or until rice is cooked. Add peas at end just long enough to heat. Sprinkle with almonds and serve.

Indian Rice with Tomatoes and Spinach

o o o

This is a mild, yet aromatic, rice dish from the Bene Israel Jewish community, near Bombay. Use fresh young spinach leaves if possible. Dhana jeera powder is a mixture of roasted and ground coriander and cumin seeds, available at Indian shops.

SERVES 6

45ml/3 tbsp vegetable
  oil
1 onion, cut in half and
  thinly sliced
400g/14oz basmati or
  American long-grain
  rice, rinsed and
  soaked in cold water
  for 30 minutes
275g/10oz young
  spinach leaves,
  cooked and squeezed
  dry, or 275g/10oz
  package frozen
  spinach, thawed and
  squeezed dry

2 medium tomatoes,
  peeled, seeded and
  diced
1.5ml/¼ tsp turmeric
5ml/1 tsp dhana jeera
  powder (see above),
  or 4ml/¾ tsp ground
  coriander and
  1.5ml/¼ tsp ground
  cumin
salt
freshly ground black
  pepper

○ In a large heavy saucepan, over medium–high heat, heat oil. Add onion and cook until softened and golden, 5–7 minutes. Drain rice well and add to onion. Cook, stirring constantly, until rice turns translucent and begins to colour, 1–2 minutes.

○ Add spinach, tomatoes, turmeric and dhana jeera powder or coriander and cumin. Add salt and pepper to taste.

○ Pour in 450ml/¾pt water and stir. Bring rice mixture to a boil, then cover tightly and reduce heat to very low. Cook until water is completely absorbed and rice is tender, 25 minutes.

○ Remove lid and fluff rice gently with a fork, being careful not to disturb the bottom layer which will have formed a crust. Cover and cook 10 minutes longer. Spoon rice into a serving bowl; scrape up browned crisp crust from bottom and spoon around the rice. Serve hot.

Pine Nuts and Currants with Rice

○ ○ ○

*P*ilau rice has infiltrated from India and Iran and from Turkey. This simple version is often served moulded to accompany main courses.

SERVES 4

85ml/3fl oz olive oil
2 small onions, finely
  chopped
60ml/4 tbsp pine nuts
30ml/2 tbsp currants
2.5ml/½ tsp saffron
  threads

450g/1lb long-grain
  rice
salt and freshly ground
  pepper
fresh parsley and
  coriander
ground paprika

○ Heat the olive oil over medium heat and sauté the chopped onions until they are limp – about 6–8 minutes. Add the pine nuts and sauté for a few minutes more, until both the onions and nuts are lightly coloured. Stir in the currants, saffron and rice, and cook for about 1 minute or until the rice is just transparent.

○ Add salt to taste and pour in water to cover, about 750ml/1¼pt. Cook, covered, on high heat until the water begins to be absorbed, then turn the heat off and allow it to sit for about 20 minutes, or until all the water is absorbed and the rice tender. If it is still not tender, add a tablespoon or so more water and simmer for a couple of minutes. Then leave to sit for a further 5 minutes.

○ If desired, press the cooked rice into a mould(s) before turning out onto a plate garnished with parsley and coriander. Dust the rice with paprika.

Trinity Rice with Almonds

○ ○ ○

*M*ade with onions, peppers and celery – the Holy Trinity of Cajun cooking – this Louisiana version of a side dish of rice pilaf has the added bonus of almonds.

SERVES 8

25g/1oz butter or olive
  oil
1 stalk celery, chopped
1 small green pepper,
  chopped
125g/4oz onion,
  chopped
2 cloves garlic, finely
  chopped
75g/3oz blanched
  almonds, slivered or
  sliced

5ml/1 tsp
  Worcestershire sauce
7.5ml/1½ tsp salt
1.5ml/¼ tsp black
  pepper
1 tomato, seeded and
  chopped
4–5 spring onions,
  chopped
30ml/2 tbsp chopped
  fresh parsley
225g/8oz white rice

○ In a medium frying pan, heat the butter or olive oil. Sauté the celery, green pepper, onion and garlic until limp, about 5 minutes.

○ Remove the vegetables and set aside. If there is no oil left in pan, add about 15ml/1 tbsp more.

○ Add the almonds, and stir until lightly browned. Add the Worcestershire sauce and stir well. Set aside.

○ In a large saucepan, bring 900ml/1½pt water to the boil. Add the salt, pepper, tomato, spring onion, parsley, sautéed vegetables and almonds and return to the boil. Add the rice, stir well and reduce the heat to very low, cover and cook until all the water is absorbed, 20–25 minutes. Or, to avoid scorching, turn off the burner and let rice cook in its own steam for the last few minutes.

RIGHT *Trinity Rice with Almonds*

Waldorf Rice Salad

o o o

SERVES 4

225g/8oz long-grain
   rice
1 small onion, peeled
   and finely chopped
6 stalks celery, washed
4 spring onions washed
   and chopped

50g/2oz walnuts,
   chopped
1 red apple
1 green apple
150ml/¼pt mayonnaise
15ml/1 tbsp parsley
juice of 1 lemon

O Cook the rice until fluffy, forking from time to time to separate the grains. Allow to cool.

O Add the finely chopped onion to the rice and mix well.

O Remove the strings from the celery stalks and chop finely. Add to the rice.

O Add the chopped spring onions and walnuts to the rice and mix well.

O Chop part of both apples into small cubes, sprinkle with lemon juice and mix with the rice salad, mayonnaise and parsley.

Risotto Milanese

o o o

This side dish from Italy can be garnished with mushrooms.

SERVES 4

15ml/1 tbsp olive oil
50g/2oz butter
1 medium onion, peeled
   and finely chopped
350g/12oz Italian
   risotto rice
750ml/1¼pt chicken
   stock

150ml/¼pt white wine
salt and freshly ground
   pepper
15ml/1 tbsp freshly
   chopped parsley
   (optional)
25g/1oz Parmesan
   cheese

O Using a heavy-bottomed saucepan, heat the oil and 25g/1oz butter. Add the onion and cook over a low heat for about 3–4 minutes without browning.

O Add the risotto rice dry and stir fry for about 2 minutes over a medium heat.

O Add half the hot chicken stock. Stir from the bottom to avoid sticking and continue to do so until the grains are separate and the stock is absorbed.

O Continue adding the remaining stock and white wine with 1 teaspoon salt bit by bit, stirring all the time, until it is all absorbed. The risotto should have cooked to a creamy consistency in about 25 minutes without becoming mushy.

O Add 25g/1oz butter and the cheese at the end of the cooking time, just before serving.

O Add the freshly ground pepper and, if you wish, a little freshly chopped parsley for flavour.

LEFT **Waldorf Rice Salad**   RIGHT **Risotto Milanese**

Spanish Rice

o o o

This is a pleasantly spicy version of Spanish Rice often served with Mexican food. The spices are briefly fried to develop their flavour, then rice is added and fried. It is then steamed in water and salsa.

MAKES 6–8 SERVINGS

45ml/3 tbsp vegetable oil
5ml/1 tsp chilli powder
2.5ml/½ tsp ground cumin
2.5ml/½ tsp dried oregano

2 cloves garlic, minced
400g/14oz white rice
250g/9oz Salsa
5ml/1 tsp salt

SALSA

MAKES 250g (9oz)

3 large tomatoes
75g/3oz finely chopped onion
2 cloves garlic, minced
2 jalapeño chillies, seeded and minced

45ml/3 tbsp finely chopped coriander
15ml/1 tbsp olive oil
15ml/1 tbsp fresh lime juice
salt to taste

O Heat the oil in a heavy frying pan. Add the chilli powder, cumin, oregano and garlic and cook for 1 minute, stirring constantly. If the oil is very hot, remove the pan from the heat and let the spices cook in the heat from the oil. After 1 minute, add the rice. Cook for 10 minutes, stirring almost constantly.

O To make the Salsa core the tomatoes, cut them in half and squeeze the seeds out. Place the tomatoes cut side down on a flameproof baking sheet and place them under the grill. (*Note:* If the baking sheet does not have sides, line it with foil, then crimp the edges to form a shallow basin to catch the tomato juice.) Grill the tomatoes until the skin is just slightly blackened and loose. Slide off their skins, drain off excess juices, and let them cool.

O While the tomatoes are cooling, mix together all the remaining ingredients. Then chop the tomatoes and add them to the Salsa. Let stand for 15 minutes or so, then taste and adjust the seasoning.

O Transfer the seasoned rice to a large pan and add 600ml/1pt water, the Salsa and salt. Bring to the boil, cover and reduce the heat. Cook until the liquid has been absorbed and the rice is tender, 20–25 minutes. Fluff with a fork. Let stand, covered, for 5 minutes, then serve.

Stuffed Sweet Peppers

o o o

This, the New World version of *chiles rellenos* made with sweet peppers, rice and meat is also popular in the Old World.

SERVES 4

3 rashers bacon, finely chopped
15ml/1 tbsp olive oil
1 small onion, chopped

225g/8oz minced beef
450g/1lb Spanish Rice
4 very large green sweet peppers

O Fry the bacon in a little oil; in the bacon fat, fry the onion and beef. When the beef is cooked, add the rice. Warm through.

O Cut the tops off the peppers. Remove the seeds and veins. Stuff the beef-bacon-rice mixture into the peppers. (Let it mound over the top if need be.) Bake in a moderately hot oven 200°C/400°F/Gas 6 until the peppers are cooked – about 30–40 minutes.

RIGHT **Spanish Rice**

Chicken and Wild Rice Salad

o o o

SERVES 4

175g/6oz long-grain
  and wild rice, cooked
225g/8oz cooked
  chicken, chopped
1 small onion, peeled
150ml/¼pt well-
  flavoured mayonnaise
125g/4oz mushrooms,
  washed

15ml/1 tbsp lemon juice
60ml/4 tbsp sweetcorn
7 black olives
salt and freshly ground
  pepper
1 lettuce
2 heads chicory

○ Cook the rice as directed on the packet of mixed long grain and wild rice. Allow to cool.

○ Add the chopped chicken to the cooled rice.

○ Chop the onion finely and add to the mixture with mayonnaise.

○ Slice the mushrooms thinly. Mix with the rice, retaining a few for the top of the salad. Pour the lemon juice over the retained mushrooms. Add the sweetcorn and 4 chopped olives to the mixture and season.

○ Arrange the lettuce and sliced chicory in the salad bowl. Turn the chicken and rice mixture into the bowl. Garnish with the mushroom slices and the 3 remaining black olives.

Thai Rice Salad

o o o

*T*his is another "leftover" dish made with rice from a previous occasion – the southern version.

SERVES 4–6

350g/12oz cooked rice
225g/8oz unsweetened
  grated coconut,
  browned in a
  350°F/180°C/Gas 4
  oven for 5–8 minutes
1 small pomelo or
  grapefruit, shredded
50g/2oz dried shrimps,
  chopped

25g/1oz bean sprouts
75g/3oz finely sliced
  lemon grass
40g/1½oz sliced green
  (string) beans
2 dried red chillies,
  pounded
15ml/1 tbsp finely
  shredded kaffir lime
  leaf

SAUCE

250ml/8fl oz water
30ml/2 tbsp chopped
  anchovies
15ml/1 tbsp palm sugar

2 kaffir lime leaves,
  torn into small pieces
1.5ml/¼ tsp sliced
  lemon grass

○ Put all the sauce ingredients in a pan, boil for 5 minutes, remove from the heat and strain. Put to one side.

○ Place the rice in half-cup moulds or large ramekins, press and invert onto a large serving platter. Arrange the rest of the raw ingredients around the edge of the rice in separate piles.

○ To eat, spoon some rice onto individual plates and take a little of each ingredient to mix with the rice according to taste. Spoon the sauce over the top.

LEFT *Chicken and Wild Rice Salad*

Egg, Cheese and Vegetable Main Dishes

Cajun Red Beans and Rice

o o o

Serve this flavourful, slow-cooked dish with the Salsa and soured cream. Extra vegetables are added near the end.

SERVES 6–8

450g/1lb dry kidney beans, picked over
45ml/3 tbsp olive oil
1 large onion, chopped
4 garlic cloves, finely chopped
2 stalks celery, chopped
1 carrot, chopped
1 green pepper, seeded and chopped
15ml/1 tbsp salt
1.5ml/¼ tsp cayenne
1.5ml/¼ tsp white pepper
1.5ml/¼ tsp black pepper
5ml/1 tsp dried thyme
7.5ml/1½ tsp ground cumin
5ml/1 tsp dry mustard
1 bay leaf
175ml/6oz can tomato purée
125ml/4fl oz dry red wine
few drops of Tabasco sauce
1 stalk celery, chopped
½ green pepper, chopped
4 spring onions, chopped
450–600g/1–1¼lb cooked rice to serve
soured cream

SALSA

2 large tomatoes, seeded and chopped
4 spring onions, chopped
½ long mild chilli, such as Anaheim or poblano
15ml/1 tbsp fresh chopped parsley
15ml/1 tbsp white wine vinegar
15ml/1 tbsp olive oil
few drops Tabasco, to taste

○ In 4.5l/1 gallon water, soak the beans at least 4 hours or overnight. Drain, rinse and return to the large pot with 1.25l/2pt water. Bring to the boil, then reduce the heat and simmer, skimming the foam, while you prepare the vegetables.

○ In a frying pan, heat the oil and sauté the onion, garlic, 2 chopped stalks celery, carrot and 1 green pepper, chopped until wilted, about 5 minutes. Add the vegetables to the beans, along with the seasonings, tomato purée and wine and continue simmering, stirring occasionally, until cooked.

○ To make the Salsa, mix all the Salsa ingredients together. Serve it with soured cream, along with the Red Bean and Rice dish.

Blue Cheese and Rice Quiche

o   o   o

SERVES 4

SHORTCRUST PASTRY

125g/4oz plain flour
a pinch of salt
25g/1oz butter or margarine

25g/1oz white fat
7.5ml/1½ tbsp cold water

FILLING

50g/2oz cooked long-grain rice
75g/3oz blue cheese, crumbled
2 eggs
30ml/2tbsp single cream
salt and freshly ground pepper

a pinch of cayenne pepper
1.5ml/¼ tsp dry mustard
10ml/2 tsp chopped parsley

O Pre-heat the oven to 200°C/400°F/Gas 6. Make up the pastry by sieving the flour and salt into a bowl. Add the fat in small lumps and rub in with the finger tips. Add the water, a few drops at a time, and mix to a firm dough. Rest in the refrigerator for 15 minutes.

O Roll the pastry out in a neat circle to fit a 18cm/7in flan ring. Lift the pastry over the ring and ease it in. Trim the top. Line with greaseproof paper and baking beans. Bake in the pre-heated oven for 15 minutes. Remove the paper and beans and cook for a further 5 minutes. Allow to cool slightly.

O Arrange the rice in the bottom of the flan. Mix the crumbled blue cheese with the rice. Beat the eggs. Add the single cream and seasonings. Pour over the rice and cheese. Sprinkle with chopped parsley. Bake for 20 minutes at the lower temperature of 180°C/350°F/Gas 4.

LEFT *Blue Cheese and Rice Quiche*

Stuffed Baked Cabbage

o   o   o

SERVES 4

8 large cabbage leaves

STUFFING

15ml/1 tbsp oil
1 large onion
125g/4oz long-grain rice

225g/8oz mushrooms
salt and pepper
1 tsp Worcestershire sauce

QUICK TOMATO SAUCE

4 spring onions, washed and chopped
425g/15oz canned peeled tomatoes
150ml/¼pt beef stock
5ml/1 tsp dried basil
1 bay leaf

bouquet garni
2 drops Tabasco sauce
2.5ml/½ tsp sugar
2.5ml/½ tsp lemon juice
10ml/2 tsp tomato purée
5ml/1 tsp cornflour
30ml/2 tbsp water

O Place the cabbage leaves in a saucepan with cold water to cover them. Bring them to the boil. Drain. Heat the oil in a frying pan. Add the onion and cook for 3 minutes over a low heat. Put the rice in 300ml/½pt boiling water with ½ teaspoon salt. Cook for 10 minutes. Rinse and drain.

O Chop the mushrooms and add to the onions to brown. Allow to cool. Add seasoning and Worcestershire sauce. Mix, then stir into the undercooked rice.

O To make up the Quick Tomato Sauce add the spring onions to the tomatoes in a saucepan. Add all ingredients except the cornflour and water. Bring to the boil and simmer for 20 minutes. After 15 minutes mix the cornflour and water and add a little hot sauce. Pour the mixture into the sauce and heat until it thickens.

O Divide the stuffing between the 8 cabbage leaves. Fold and secure with cocktail sticks. Place in an ovenproof dish and pour the tomato sauce over. Bake at 180°C/350°F/Gas 4 for 25 minutes. Remove the bouquet garni, bay leaf and cocktail sticks before serving.

Rice à la Provençale

∘ ∘ ∘

This is a useful recipe to serve with many main dishes as there is no need to cook separate vegetables.

SERVES 5

225g/8oz long-grain rice
600ml/1pt water
2.5ml/½ tsp salt
60ml/4 tbsp oil
25g/1oz butter
2 onions, peeled and
    finely chopped
2 cloves garlic, crushed
salt and freshly ground
    black pepper
2 red peppers, seeded
    and blanched

4 courgettes, washed
    and thinly sliced
2.5ml/½ tsp basil
60ml/4 tbsp white wine
8 tomatoes, skinned
    and chopped
15ml/1 tbsp chopped
    capers
2 hard-boiled eggs
8 green olives, stoned
30ml/2 tbsp chopped
    parsley or chervil

○ Cook the long-grain rice in 600ml/1pt water with ½ teaspoon salt, by bringing the water to the boil, adding the rice and stirring to separate the grains. Cover and simmer gently until the water has all been absorbed, which will take about 15 minutes.

○ Heat the oil and butter and cook the onions over a low heat for about 4 minutes.

○ Add the garlic. Dice the blanched peppers and add with the sliced courgettes, the basil and white wine. Stir gently until cooked for about 5 minutes. Lastly stir in the tomatoes. Gently fold in the cooked rice and season well.

○ Add the chopped capers and turn into a heated serving dish.

○ Decorate with hard-boiled eggs, green olives and chopped herbs.

Vegetable Pilaf

∘ ∘ ∘

SERVES 4

50g/2oz butter
1 medium onion, peeled
    and thinly sliced
225g/8oz long-grain
    rice

salt and freshly ground
    pepper
a pinch of saffron or a
    few drops of yellow
    food colouring
450ml/¾pt stock

○ Use an ovenproof casserole for cooking this dish. Heat 40g/1½oz butter and cook the onion over a low heat for 4 minutes. Add the rice and stir for another 3 minutes.

○ Season well. Add the saffron or colouring to the stock. Then pour the stock on to the rice and mix well with a fork. Bring to the boil. Cover and cook in the oven at 180°C/350°F/Gas 4 for about 15 minutes until stock is absorbed and rice grains are separate.

○ Add the remaining butter and, if you wish, 1 tablespoon grated cheese.

○ Another version of this savoury rice can be made by adding mushrooms, peppers or grated carrot to the onion.

RIGHT *Rice à la Provençale*

Meaty Main Dishes

Marinated Lamb Chops with Savoury Rice

○ ○ ○

SERVES 4

8 best end of neck chops

MARINADE

30ml/2 tbsp oil
30ml/2 tbsp soya sauce
5ml/1 tsp brown sugar

salt and freshly ground pepper
5ml/1 tsp lemon juice

SAUCE

1 onion, peeled
30ml/2 tbsp sherry
30ml/2 tbsp water
30ml/2 tbsp redcurrant jelly
4ml/¼ tbsp ground coriander

125g/4oz canned pineapple pieces
15ml/1 tbsp parsley, chopped
225g/8oz Savoury Rice (see Rice Ring, pages 44–5)

○ Place the chops in a plastic bag with the mixed marinade. Allow to soak for several hours. Turn the bag around on a dish to help the meat to contact the marinade.

○ Pre-heat the oven to 200°C/400°F/Gas 6.

○ Arrange the chops on a rack over a roasting pan and place in the pre-heated oven. Cook for 15–20 minutes.

○ Make the sauce by adding 1 tablespoon oil to a saucepan and cooking the finely chopped onion for 3 minutes. Add the remainder of the marinade from the chops and simmer for a few minutes. Add the sherry, water, redcurrant jelly, coriander, seasoning and pineapple pieces. Simmer for 15 minutes. The sauce may be blended before serving. Alternatively mix 1 teaspoon cornflour with 1 tablespoon water, add a little warmed sauce and return to the saucepan. Stir until sauce is slightly thickened.

○ Lay the chops on a bed of savoury rice, sprinkled with chopped parsley. Pour sauce as you like.

Madras Beef Curry

○ ○ ○

*C*urries are best made in advance as the spicy flavour improves with reheating. This curry can be cooked on top of the cooker but remember to check from time to time that it is not sticking or drying out. Add a little stock or water if necessary.

SERVES 4

90ml/6 tbsp vegetable
  oil
2 large onions, peeled
4 stalks celery, washed
650g/1½lb chuck steak
15ml/1 tbsp flour
2.5ml/½ tsp paprika
2.5ml/½ tsp garam
  masala
15–30ml/1–2 tbsp
  Madras curry
  powder

1 bay leaf
5ml/1 tsp tomato purée
600ml/1pt beef stock or
  water
425g/15oz canned
  peeled tomatoes
1 medium potato,
  peeled
onion rings
15ml/1 tbsp chopped
  parsley

○ Heat 4 tablespoons oil in a large frying pan. Cut off a few thin onion rings for garnish, and then finely chop the remainder and cook for 5 minutes.

○ Remove the strings from the celery and chop finely. Add to the onions and stir well for a further 2 minutes. Remove to a casserole or thick-bottomed saucepan.

○ Trim the steak and remove any gristle. Cut into 2.5cm/1in cubes. Sprinkle with flour, seasoned with the paprika and garam masala. Add remaining oil to the frying pan and fry the meat until golden on all sides. Remove with a slotted spoon to the casserole.

○ Sprinkle the curry powder and any remaining flour into the pan and simmer for 2 minutes. Add the tomato purée to the stock and pour into the pan, stirring well to remove meat juices. Add the canned tomatoes and bring to the boil.

○ Meanwhile cut the potato into cubes and bring to the boil for 5 minutes in salted water.

○ Add the tomato and curry mixture to the meat and onions. Stir well.

○ Drain the potato cubes and add to the casserole with ½ teaspoon salt. Cook in the oven at 180°C/350°F/Gas 4 for 1 hour or until the meat is tender. Taste and season.

○ Serve with pilau or pilaf rice, mango chutney and poppadoms or any of the other side dishes or sambals which are so popular with curry.

Souvlakia with Rice

o o o

This dish is delicious when cooked on a barbecue.

SERVES 4

450g/1lb leg of lamb
12 bay leaves
juice of ½ a lemon
2 tbsp olive oil

salt and freshly ground
  pepper
5ml/1 tsp oregano
225–275g/8–10oz long-
  grain rice, cooked

○ Allow one skewer for each person. Cut the lamb into
2.5cm/1in cubes and thread onto the skewers with pieces
of bay leaf in between. Leave space at either end of the
skewers to enable them to rest on the grill rack.

○ Beat the lemon juice into the olive oil, season with
salt, pepper and oregano and leave the lamb to marinate
in the mixture in a plastic bag for at least 1 hour.

○ Cook under a hot grill for about 10 minutes turning
occasionally, so that the lamb becomes well seared on the
outside and tender and juicy inside.

○ Serve immediately with a tomato and cucumber salad,
quarters of lemon to squeeze over the meat and a dish of
cooked rice. Serve lemon juice or seasoned yoghurt on all
types of accompanying salads.

LEFT **Madras Beef Curry**

Red Beans and Rice with Tasso and Andouille

o   o   o

*T*he use of two highly spiced meats means this is a spicy dish. You can substitute ham hocks for Tasso, but increase the amount of cayenne and black pepper.

SERVES 6–8

450g/1lb dried kidney
  beans, picked over
30–60ml/2–4 tbsp
  vegetable oil (or
  bacon drippings)
450g/1lb chopped onion
4 stalks celery, chopped
2½ green peppers,
  chopped
2 cloves garlic, finely
  chopped
225g/8oz Tasso, cubed
225g/8oz Andouille
  sausage, sliced
2 bay leaves
10ml/2 tsp salt
10ml/2 tsp ground cumin

5ml/1 tsp dry mustard
15ml/1 tbsp chopped
  fresh oregano or 1
  tsp dried
1.5ml/¼ tsp black
  pepper
1.5ml/¼ tsp cayenne
225g/8oz spring onion,
  chopped
1 stalk celery, chopped
½ green pepper,
  chopped
45ml/3 tbsp chopped
  fresh parsley
600–650g/1¼–1½lb
  cooked rice to serve

O In 4.5l/1gal water, soak the beans at least 4 hours. Drain, rinse and return to the large pot with 1.25l/2¼pt water. Bring to the boil, then simmer, skimming the foam, while you prepare the vegetables.

O In a frying pan, heat the oil and sauté the 450g/1lb onion, 4 chopped stalks celery, the green peppers and garlic until wilted, about 5 minutes. Add the vegetables to the beans, along with the Tasso, sausage and seasonings and continue simmering, stirring occasionally, until beans are tender, 1–1½ hours. Add extra water if necessary. Taste and adjust seasonings.

O Just before serving, stir in the last measure of spring onions, celery, green pepper and parsley. Serve over rice.

Albondiguitas
(Mexican Meatballs) with Salsa

○   ○   ○

The meatballs that make up the famous Albondigas Soup are prepared in a number of other ways. If they are deep-fried, they can be served on their own as a snack or as a meat dish; or with a tomato sauce; or even in a boleta (Mexican roll) to make a torta, the Mexican equivalent of the American "submarine" sandwich.

SERVES 6–8

450g/1lb lean minced beef
350g/12oz minced pork
125g/4oz cooked rice
1 small onion, chopped very finely

2 cloves garlic, chopped very finely
2 eggs
chopped coriander (optional)
salt and pepper to taste
lard or oil for frying

SALSA DI JICAMATE
(BASIC TOMATO SAUCE)

650g/24oz can tomatoes, chopped
175g/6oz can tomato purée
2 large onions, finely chopped
5–10 cloves garlic
2–4 serrano chillies
200ml/6.5fl oz red wine or sherry
pinch each of parsley, sage, rosemary, thyme, oregano

salt and pepper to taste
olive oil for frying
sugar if necessary
coriander

○   To make the meatballs mix all the meatball ingredients together thoroughly. Form the mixture into balls: for a main course, rather smaller than a golf-ball, for appetizers, about 2–3cm/1in in diameter. Mexican cooks often insert a piece of hard-boiled egg or half an olive in the middle.

○   Deep-fry for several minutes – it takes a while for the centre to be cooked fully. Serve with the Salsa Di Jicamate sauce. You can either fry the meatballs first, or poach them in the sauce.

○   To make the salsa sauce fry the onions and garlic in 2–3 tablespoons of oil. When they are soft and golden, add the serranos, tomatoes, tomato purée, wine, spices and seasoning. Add sugar if the sauce is too sharp; this will depend on the wine and the tomatoes, and often you won't need sugar. Simmer for 15–30 minutes; add the coriander a minute or two before the end of cooking.

○   You can omit the wine; if you do, omit the tomato purée as well.

Creole Curried Pork Chops
with Rice Pilaf

o   o   o

This is a subtly seasoned jerk dish that complements
the curried rice. Add a tossed salad for a meal that can
be put together in less than half an hour.

SERVES 4

200g/7oz long-grain
    white rice
30ml/2 tbsp vegetable
    oil
175g/6oz raisins
2.5ml/½ tsp ground
    cumin
2.5ml/½ tsp salt
2.5ml/½ tsp freshly
    ground black pepper
300ml/10fl oz chicken
    stock

50ml/2fl oz water
7.5ml/1½ tsp curry
    powder
.75ml/⅛ tsp ground
    cinnamon
.75ml/⅛ tsp chilli
    powder
8 very thin pork chops
    (1kg/2lb in total)

O Toast the rice in 15ml/1 tbsp oil in a saucepan for 2–3
minutes until golden. Stir in the raisins, ¼ tsp cumin, salt
and pepper. Cook for 1 minute. Add the stock and water.
Simmer, covered, until the liquids are absorbed by the
rice, about 15–20 minutes.

O Meanwhile, combine the curry powder, remaining
cumin, cinnamon and chilli powder. Rub on the chops.

O Divide the remaining oil between two large frying
pans and heat to moderately hot. Divide the chops
between the frying pans and cook, covered, for 3 minutes
on each side until cooked through. Alternatively, cook in
two stages in one frying pan, keeping the first batch of
chops warm. Serve with the rice.

Sausage and Bacon Rolls
with Tomato Rice

○ ○ ○

SERVES 4

225g/8oz long-grain
   rice
600ml/1pt beef stock
10ml/2 tsp tomato
   purée
1 small onion, peeled
   and chopped

2.5ml/½ tsp salt
8 sausages
8 rashers bacon
300ml/½pt Spicy
   Tomato Sauce

SPICY TOMATO SAUCE

5ml/1 tsp oil
1 onion, peeled and
   finely chopped
1 chilli pepper seeded
   (optional)
1 clove garlic, crushed
1 carrot, scraped and
   grated

200g/7oz canned peeled
   tomatoes
150ml/¼pt stock or
   water
1 bay leaf
2.5ml/½ tsp oregano

○ Wash the long-grain rice several times and drain.

○ Mix the beef stock, tomato purée and onion with the salt and bring to the boil. Pour over the rice and fork through to stop grains sticking together. Cover and simmer until all liquid is absorbed, about 15 minutes.

○ To make the Spicy Tomato Sauce heat the oil in a saucepan and cook over a low heat for 4 minutes. Add the garlic and grated carrot. Stir well and then add remaining ingredients. Season well. Simmer for at least 20 minutes on a low heat.

○ Turn the grill on high and brown the sausages on each side for 3 minutes. Allow to cool slightly and then wrap bacon rashers around the sausages.

○ Grill for a further 5 minutes under a medium heat. Alternatively cook in the oven in the tomato sauce at 180°C/350°F/Gas 4 for 15 minutes after browning under the grill.

○ Arrange sausage and bacon rolls on the tomato rice and pour the sauce on top.

Alma-ata Pilaf

o o o

There are numerous pilaf recipes originating in Central Asia; this one from the capital of Kazakhstan utilizes the rich bounty of fruit which grow there – the apples are particularly famous.

SERVES 6

100g/3½oz blanched slivered almonds
60ml/4 tbsp vegetable oil
450g/1 lb lamb steaks, cubed
2 large carrots, cut into julienne strips
2 large onions, thinly sliced
9–10 dried apricots, chopped
90ml/6 tbsp raisins

650g/1½lb long-grained white rice
salt and freshly ground black pepper
450ml/¾pt chicken stock
150ml/¼pt orange juice
5ml/1 tsp grated orange rind
600ml/1pt water
1 medium red apple, cored and chopped

O Preheat the oven to 200°C/400°F/Gas 6. Scatter the almonds on a baking sheet and toast in the oven until golden, about 5 minutes. Set aside and turn the oven down to 180°C/350°F/Gas 4.

O Heat the oil in a large frying pan over medium–high heat. When just smoking, add the lamb cubes and sauté for 6 minutes, or until well browned. Transfer the meat with a slotted spoon to a large casserole.

O Turn the heat down slightly and sauté the carrots in the oil for 3 minutes, stirring, then add the onions and continue to sauté for another 6 minutes, until the onions are soft and lightly coloured. Stir in the dried apricots, raisins, and rice. Cook for 2 minutes until the rice is coated with the oil and is becoming opaque.

O Add the rice mixture to the casserole with the meat. Season to taste, then pour over the chicken stock, orange juice and rind, and water. Bring to the boil, then cover the casserole and transfer it to the oven. Bake for 40 minutes, or until all the liquid is absorbed.

O Remove the pilaf from the oven, stir in the chopped apple, and transfer it to a large serving dish, making a neat mound. Scatter the toasted almonds over the top and serve.

Beef Saté

o o o

SERVES 4

2 spring onions,
  washed
2.5cm/1in fresh root
  ginger, grated
2 cloves garlic, crushed
8 cardamom pods
5ml/1 tsp cumin seeds

5ml/1 tsp coriander
  seeds
juice of 1 lemon
5ml/1 tsp grated or
  ground nutmeg
2 bay leaves
30ml/2 tbsp oil
675g/1½lb rump steak

SATÉ SAUCE

90ml/6 tbsp peanut
  butter
15ml/1 tbsp brown
  sugar
2 chilli peppers, seeded
5ml/1 tsp sugar

juice and rind of
  1 lemon
150ml/¼pt beef stock
225g/8oz long-grain
  rice, cooked

O Place all the ingredients except the meat in a blender to make a paste.

O Trim the meat and cut into small squares. Mix with the paste and allow to marinate for several hours.

O Arrange the meat on skewers.

O Make the sauce by mixing all the ingredients except the lemon juice together in a saucepan. Bring to the boil and simmer for about 20 minutes. Add the lemon juice.

O While the sauce is cooking turn the grill onto a high heat and allow the skewered meat to cook. Turn every 2 minutes for the first 6 minutes, then lower the heat and continue cooking. The time will depend on whether you like your meat slightly rare or well cooked.

O Accompany with boiled rice.

Mexican Roast Pork with with Chorizo-Rice Stuffing

○ ○ ○

Roast pork is stuffed with a spicy stuffing, then spread with salsa and roasted. Fiery salsas infuse the meat with the heat of the chillies, while milder salsas let the other flavours show through.

SERVES 6

1.5ml/¼ tsp salt
10ml/2 tsp olive oil or butter
200g/7oz white rice
175–225g/6–8oz chorizo sausage

75g/3oz chopped onion
2 cloves garlic, minced
40g/1½oz toasted pine nuts (see opposite)
1kg/2lb pork loin
300g/11oz salsa

This simple cooked salsa is good with corn chips or as a sauce over eggs or Mexican food. With a few jalapeño seeds included, it is fairly hot. You may use unpeeled tomatoes, but if you wish to remove the skin, dip the tomatoes in boiling water for 30 seconds. The skins should slip off easily.

SALSA
MAKES ABOUT 500G/18OZ

450g/1lb seeded, chopped tomatoes
2 cloves minced garlic
75g/3oz finely chopped onion
4 jalapeño chillies, chopped, with some seeds included

15ml/1 tbsp cider vinegar
5ml/1 tsp fresh oregano or 1.5ml/¼ tsp dried
salt to taste

○ Preheat the oven to 180°C/350°F/Gas 4. Put 475ml/16fl oz water in a saucepan, add the salt and olive oil or butter and bring to the boil. Stir in the rice, cover and reduce the heat. Cook until the water has been absorbed and the rice is tender, 15–20 minutes.

○ To make the Salsa, in a medium saucepan, simmer the tomatoes, garlic and onion for 10–15 minutes, uncovered, to evaporate excess liquid from the tomatoes. Add the jalapeños, vinegar and oregano, and simmer for 5 minutes more. Add salt to taste. Set aside.

○ Crumble the chorizo into a small frying pan. Brown over medium heat, 7–10 minutes, then set aside. Discard all but 1 tbsp of fat. Reheat the fat and add the onion. Sauté for 5 minutes, then add the garlic and pine nuts, and cook for 1 minute. Remove from the heat. Mix the chorizo and the onion mixture into the cooked rice.

○ Unroll the pork loin, or make several lengthwise cuts so that it opens as much as possible into a thick, flat piece. Spoon some rice mixture into the centre of the loin, then reroll the meat and tie with string. You will have some rice left over. Put it in a lightly greased baking dish, cover and set aside.

○ Put the pork, cut side up, on a rack in a small roasting tin. Spread some of the Salsa over the pork, but make sure you have some left over for basting. Put the pork in the oven and cook for approximately 1 hour, until the internal temperature measured with a meat thermometer reaches 71°C/160°F (although the meat is safe at 60°C/140°F). Baste the meat at least once with the additional Salsa. During the last 5 minutes of cooking, put the leftover rice stuffing in the oven.

○ When the pork is done, remove it from the oven and let stand for 15 minutes before carving it into slices. Let the stuffing continue to cook while the pork rests.

○ To toast pine nuts: spread them in a single layer on a baking sheet. Bake at 180°C/350°F/Gas 4 for 5–10 minutes until they are golden brown. Watch pine nuts carefully as they burn very quickly.

Liver and Rice Casserole

○   ○   ○

The baking oven came from the east more than a thousand years ago. The old, tried and true Finnish dishes still depend on the oven. In fact, most Finnish cooking makes heavy use of the oven.

SERVES 6–8

400g/14oz white long grain rice	125g/4oz raisins
3.25 l/6pt boiling salted water	30ml/2 tbsp golden syrup
40g/1½oz butter	10ml/2 tsp salt
1 medium onion, finely chopped	5ml/1 tsp white pepper
450ml/¾pt milk	5ml/1 tsp dried oregano
2 eggs, lightly beaten	650g/1½lb calf's or ox liver, minced
4 slices of streaky bacon, cooked and diced	

○ Cook the rice in the boiling salted water for about 12 minutes, then drain and put aside.

○ Melt 25g/1oz butter in a frying pan and gently sauté the onion until golden. Remove and put aside.

○ Preheat the oven to 170°C/325°F/Gas 3. In a large bowl, carefully combine the cooked rice, the milk and beaten eggs. Add the onion, diced bacon, raisins and golden syrup. Season with salt, pepper and oregano. Stir in the minced liver and mix thoroughly.

○ Grease an ovenproof dish and add the liver and rice mixture. Bake, uncovered, for 1–1½ hours. Serve with green salad and loganberry or cranberry sauce.

Coconut Beef Curry

○ ○ ○

𝒯his is one of the driest of Thai curries, and usually quite fiery.

SERVES 8

50ml/2fl oz peanut or corn oil
300g/11oz beef sirloin, cut in 3 x 1.5 x 1cm/1¼ x ¾ x ½in pieces
675ml/24fl oz thin coconut milk

15ml/1 tbsp fish sauce
10ml/2 tsp sugar
2 fresh red chillies, sliced
2 kaffir lime leaves, sliced finely
20g/¾oz sweet basil leaves

CURRY PASTE

6 dried red chillies, chopped roughly
7 white peppercorns
40g/1½oz garlic, chopped roughly
25g/1oz shallots, chopped roughly
2 coriander roots, chopped roughly

10ml/2 tsp salt
5ml/1 tsp roughly chopped galangal
5ml/1 tsp roughly chopped lemon grass
5ml/1 tsp roughly chopped kaffir lime zest
5ml/1 tsp shrimp paste

○ Pound all the curry paste ingredients together with a mortar and pestle or in a blender to form a paste.

○ Heat the oil in a pan or wok and fry the curry paste for 3–4 minutes. Add the beef and fry for 2 minutes, then add the coconut milk and boil until the beef is tender, about 15 minutes. Add the fish sauce, sugar and chilli. Remove from the heat, transfer to a serving plate and sprinkle with the lime zest and basil.

○ Serve accompanied by rice.

Sweet and Sour Pork with Rice

○ ○ ○

SERVES 4

450g/1lb leg of pork, cut in a thick slice
1 small onion, peeled and sliced
2.5cm/1in fresh root ginger, finely chopped
1 clove garlic

15ml/1 tbsp dry sherry
30ml/2 tbsp soya sauce
salt and freshly ground pepper
oil for frying
225–275g/8–10oz boiled rice

SAUCE

1 small red pepper, seeded
1 small green pepper, seeded
2 spring onions, washed
150ml/½pt chicken stock

15ml/1 tbsp white wine vinegar
30ml/2 tsp brown sugar
15ml/1 tbsp tomato purée
10ml/2 tsp cornflour

BATTER

45ml/3 tbsp cornflour
10ml/2 tsp water

1 egg

LEFT AND ABOVE *Sweet and Sour Pork with Rice*

○ Cut the pork into 2.5cm/1in cubes after trimming.

○ Mix up the marinade of onion, ginger, garlic, sherry, soya sauce and seasoning and allow the pork to stand in this for at least 1 hour, turning from time to time.

○ Cut the peppers into 1cm/½in cubes and chop the spring onions into thick rings.

○ Place all other ingredients, apart from the cornflour, into a saucepan with the peppers and spring onions. Mix the cornflour with 2 tablespoons of cold water and mix into saucepan. Fry the meat before heating the sauce.

○ Make up the batter in a deep plate, mixing the cornflour, water and egg together until thick.

○ Drop the drained marinated meat into the batter. Make sure the fat is very hot (170°C/360°F) before dropping the meat in, either with tongs or a slotted spoon. Cook for about 2–4 minutes until golden. Drain.

○ Heat the sweet and sour sauce and, when thickened, add the fried pork. Accompany with plain boiled rice.

Pork Stuffed Cabbage Leaves

○ ○ ○

$\mathcal{K}$nown as gotabki in Poland, these may be filled with pork or lamb, rice, a combination of both or with buckwheat. Gotabki may be made using very large cabbage leaves, serving just one per portion with a little unthickened cooking liquid poured over. Alternatively, they may be dressed with a tomato or béchamel-type sauce. Here the cooking juices are thickened and soured cream is added to make a delicious sauce.

SERVES 4

8 large green cabbage
   leaves
1 onion, finely chopped
25g/1oz butter
125g/4oz cooked pork
   or lamb, diced
125g/4oz long-grain
   rice, cooked and
   cooled
125g/4oz mushrooms,
   chopped (use
   chestnut mushrooms
   for a good flavour)

2.5ml/½ tsp dried
   oregano
30ml/2 tbsp chopped
   fresh parsley
salt and freshly ground
   black pepper
250ml/8fl oz stock,
   such as chicken or
   beef
30ml/2 tbsp plain flour
30ml/2 tbsp water
150ml/¼pt soured
   cream

○ Cook the cabbage in boiling water for 2–3 minutes, until pliable. Drain well, dry on absorbent kitchen paper towel and trim away a small "V" shape from any hard stalks.

○ Cook the onion in the butter for 10 minutes, until soft. Stir in the meat, rice, mushrooms, herbs and seasoning. Mix well and cook for 1 minute. Roughly divide this filling into eight.

○ Place a portion of filling on each leaf, slightly nearer the stalk end than in the middle. Fold the stalk end over the filling, then fold the sides of the leaf over. Roll the stuffing and leaf from the stalk end to make a neat parcel. Put into a medium saucepan, join down. Stuff the other leaves and pack them fairly tightly into the pan. If the pan is too large to hold the leaves, use a smaller one. Pour in the stock and heat until simmering. Cover and cook for 20 minutes.

○ Transfer the gotabki to a warmed serving dish. Blend the flour with the water and stir into the cooking liquid. Bring to the boil, stirring, then add the soured cream and stir until hot. Taste for seasoning, pour this sauce over the gotabki and serve.

Crown Roast of Lamb with Apricot Rice Stuffing

○ ○ ○

This is an excellent dinner party dish as it can be prepared in advance.

SERVES 6

2 best ends of neck (lamb)	*15ml/1 tbsp oil*
	freshly ground pepper

STUFFING

125g/4oz long-grain or risotto rice	*15ml/1 tbsp sultanas*
15ml/1 tbsp butter	*15ml/1 tbsp chopped mixed nuts*
1 onion, peeled and finely chopped	*1 egg, beaten*
2 stalks of celery	*15ml/1 tbsp chopped parsley*
125g/4oz dried apricots, steeped or 1 large can apricots	*salt and freshly ground pepper*

○ Ask the butcher to prepare the crown roast or, if this is not possible, have the best ends chined. Remove the skin from the fatty side of the joints. Cut along the fat about 3.5cm/1½in from the top of the bone and remove fat and meat from the tops of the bones. Scrape the little end bones clean with a knife. Turn the meat over the cut between the cutlets to enable the joint to bend.

○ Stand the two pieces of meat up with the bones at the top. Turn fatty sides in and sew together at the top and bottom of the joins to make the crown roast. Paint over with oil and sprinkle with pepper.

○ For the stuffing, partially cook the rice for 10 minutes, rinse and allow to drain and cool.

○ Heat the butter and oil and cook the onion for 4 minutes over a low heat. Add the chopped celery, chopped apricots (if using canned apricots retain 8 drained halves for garnish), sultanas and nuts. Lastly stir

in the rice. Turn into a bowl and allow to cool. Mix with the egg yolk and parsley.

○ Fill the centre of the roast with the stuffing. Cover with a piece of foil.

○ Cover the individual tips of the bones with foil to prevent charring. Then completely cover with foil. Roast in the oven at 180°C/350°F/Gas 4 for 1½–2 hours, depending on size of the cutlets.

○ Any excess stuffing may be used to stuff apricot halves which can be cooked brushed with oil for the last 30 minutes of cooking time.

○ Remove the crown roast to a heated plate and make gravy to accompany roast in the usual way. If using canned apricots, a little juice may be added to the gravy. Remove the string before carving through the cutlets.

Mexican Chilli

○ ○ ○

SERVES 4

2 onions, peeled
3 stalks celery, washed
30ml/2 tbsp vegetable oil
2 cloves garlic, crushed
450g/1lb lean minced
   beef
425g/15oz canned
   peeled tomatoes
1 carrot, scraped
5–10ml/1–2 tsp chilli
   powder

1 fresh chilli pepper,
   seeded
1 green pepper, seeded
425g/15oz can kidney
   beans
1 bouquet garni
300ml/½pt stock
225g/8oz long-grain
   rice

○ Chop the onions finely and remove strings from the celery before chopping into thin slices.

○ Heat the oil in a frying pan and cook the onions, celery and garlic over a low heat for 5 minutes.

○ In a thick-bottomed saucepan heat 1 tablespoon oil over a medium heat and brown the minced beef, stirring to keep the meat in small pieces.

○ When the meat is evenly browned add the cooked onion mixture and the whole can of tomatoes, including juice.

○ Grate the carrot and add to the meat mixture. Add the chilli powder, finely chopped chilli pepper and diced green pepper. Finally add the kidney beans and bouquet garni. Mix well with stock and allow to simmer gently for 40 minutes.

○ Cook the rice by the absorption method (see page 10).

Lamb Tikka with Pilau Rice

o o o

SERVES 4

600g/1¼lb leg of lamb
 (cut in a thick slice)
150ml/¼pt natural
 yoghurt
5ml/1 tsp chilli powder
5ml/1 tsp crushed
 coriander
5ml/1 tsp garam
 masala
2.5ml/½ tsp salt
juice of 1 fresh lime or
 lemon

225g/8oz pilau rice,
 cooked
8 lettuce leaves
2 tomatoes, sliced
12 slices of cucumber
1 small onion, peeled
 and finely diced
1 lemon or lime,
 quartered
2 rosemary sprigs

O Leg of lamb sliced about 1cm/½in thick is best for this dish. Remove any bone or gristle. Cut into 1cm/½in thick cubes.

O Mix yoghurt with all other ingredients in a plastic bag or a flat dish. Add the meat to the marinade and allow to soak for several hours. Turn from time to time.

O Divide the meat onto 4 skewers and cook under a hot grill, turning every two minutes.

O Serve each portion off the skewer with pilau rice and garnish with a green salad.

Red Bean Pork and Rice

o o o

*F*rom Central America to the Caribbean to New Orleans, slow-cooked and highly seasoned red beans and rice is a traditional dish. This main-course version uses leftover pork, but it's good with chunks of sausage or shreds of barbecued brisket too. Top with uncooked salsa for colour, crunch and flavour.

SERVES 6–8

350g/12oz dried kidney
   beans
30–45ml/2–3 tbsp
   vegetable oil
175g/6oz chopped onion
2 stalks celery, chopped
3 cloves garlic, minced
275g/10oz cooked pork
   (diced ham, slivers of
   ham hocks, shredded,
   barbecued or roast
   pork)

2 bay leaves
5ml/1 tsp ground
   cumin
2.5ml/½ tsp pepper
5–10ml/1–2 tsp salt
750g/1¾lb cooked rice
350g/12oz Salsa Cruda
soured cream

SALSA CRUDA

MAKES ABOUT 200G/7OZ

4 medium tomatoes,
  cored and halved
175g/6oz chopped
  onion
5 serrano chillies,
  partly seeded if
  desired, minced

2 cloves garlic, minced
45ml/3 tbsp chopped
  fresh coriander
30ml/2 tbsp fresh lime
  juice
15ml/1 tbsp olive oil
1.5–2.5ml/¼–½ tsp salt

○ To make the Red Bean Pork pick through the beans for pebbles or other debris. Put the beans in a large saucepan, add water and soak overnight. Or you can bring the beans and water to the boil, boil for 2 minutes, then cover, turn off the heat, and let the beans stand for an hour.

○ To make the Salsa Cruda cut the tomatoes in half and squeeze out seeds. Grill the tomatoes cut side down on a flameproof baking sheet until skins are partly blackened and skins slip off easily. Remove from heat. Let them cool in a colander so excess liquids drain off and then remove the skins. Purée in a blender or food processor, but do not purée so long that the tomato becomes liquefied.

○ Stir all the remaining ingredients together and add the tomatoes. Let stand for 30 minutes, then taste and adjust the seasoning.

○ Drain and rinse the beans and put them back in the pan. Add enough water to cover the beans by about 5cm/2in then bring to the boil. Meanwhile prepare the vegetables. Heat the oil in a frying pan. Add the onion and celery and cook for 5 minutes, then add the garlic and cook for 2 minutes longer. Add the vegetables to the beans, along with the pork, bay leaves, cumin and pepper. Reduce the heat and simmer until the beans are tender, 1–1½ hours. Check periodically and add more water if needed. Taste and add salt.

○ Serve the beans over rice, topped with the Salsa Cruda and with soured cream if desired.

Spanish Pork and Spinach Rice

○ ○ ○

"Sloppy" rice, caldoso, is the Spanish name for this type of dish, which is much easier to make than paella.

SERVES 4–6

350–450g/12oz–1lb
  lean pork, cubed
90ml/6 tbsp olive oil
salt and freshly ground
  black pepper
250g/9oz fresh spinach,
  washed, trimmed and
  chopped
8 young garlic or
  whites of fat green
  onions

4 tomatoes, chopped
10ml/2 tsp paprika
375g/13oz paella or
  risotto rice
pinch of saffron
  strands
1.5l/2½pt light broth or
  water, warmed

○ Heat the oil in a paella pan or wide shallow casserole and fry the seasoned pork cubes. When they are golden, spread the chopped spinach over the top and cover with another paella pan, lid or baking sheet.

○ When the spinach has thoroughly wilted, add the garlic or whites of the green onions and the chopped tomatoes, sprinkling them with the paprika. Cook gently until the tomatoes have reduced. Meanwhile, rinse the rice, drain and add it with some salt to the pan and stir.

○ Powder the saffron into the warm broth with your fingers and bring to a gentle simmer. Cook over low heat for 15–18 minutes, until the rice is done. Check the seasoning and stir.

Thai Beef with Spinach

o o o

SERVES 4

650g/1½lb chuck steak
300ml/½pt coconut milk
5ml/1 tsp brown sugar
15ml/1 tbsp soya sauce
15ml/1 tbsp mixed
    chopped nuts
2 cloves garlic, crushed
1 onion, peeled
2.5cm/1in fresh root
    ginger

2 fresh chilli peppers,
    seeded
salt and freshly ground
    pepper, seeded
juice of ½ lemon
15ml/1 tbsp cornflour
450g/1lb frozen
    spinach or 1kg/2lb
    fresh spinach
60ml/4 tbsp yoghurt

O Trim off excess fat from the meat, and cut into thin strips.

O Put the coconut milk, sugar, nuts and soya sauce into a saucepan. Mix the beef with these ingredients and bring to the boil. Immediately the mixture bubbles, turn the heat down and allow to simmer for about 10 minutes.

O In a blender or food processor make a paste with the garlic, onion, fresh ginger, chilli peppers, a little salt and lemon juice. Mix this paste with the cornflour and a little cold water. Add some of the hot liquid from the beef to the mixture before stirring into the beef. Cover and simmer gently for about 30–40 minutes until meat is cooked.

O Cook the spinach as directed on the packet if using frozen. For fresh spinach wash and remove large stems and cook in a small amount of boiling salted water for about 5 minutes. Drain cooking water into a bowl and use to adjust sauce if it has reduced too much. Arrange drained spinach in a hot serving dish.

O Put beef onto the spinach and trickle yoghurt on top.

O Serve with plain boiled rice.

Pineapple Sweet-Sour Pork Balls

o o o

SERVES 4

450g/1lb minced pork	1 egg
5ml/1 tsp sesame oil	45ml/3 tbsp soya sauce
90ml/6 tbsp cornflour	45ml/3 tbsp oil

SWEET AND SOUR SAUCE

5ml/1 tsp cornflour	225g/8oz can pineapple
90ml/6 tbsp dry sherry	chunks in syrup
90ml/6 tbsp soya sauce	1 large onion, cut in
60ml/4 tbsp tomato	chunks
purée	1 large green bell
60ml/4 tbsp sugar	pepper, cut in chunks
45ml/3 tbsp white wine	2 carrots, cut in
vinegar	2.5cm/1in strips

○ Pound the pork with the sesame oil until well mixed, then mix in the cornflour, egg and soya sauce in the same way. Have a plate ready to hold the pork balls. Wash, then wet your hands under cold water. Take small portions of the meat mixture, about the size of walnuts, and knead them into balls. Keep wetting your hands as this prevents the meat from sticking to them, and it gives the balls an even surface.

○ Before cooking the pork balls, start preparing the sauce: blend the cornflour to a paste with 6 tablespoons water. Add the sherry and soya sauce, then stir in the tomato purée, sugar and vinegar. Drain the liquid from the pineapple into the mixture.

○ Heat the oil and stir-fry the pork balls until evenly browned and cooked through. Use a draining spoon to remove them from the pan.

○ Add the onion, pepper and carrots to the hot fat and stir-fry these ingredients for about 5 minutes, until slightly softened. Give the liquid sauce mixture a stir, then pour it into the pan and bring to a boil, stirring all the time. Stir in the pork balls and pineapple and cook, stirring over reduced heat for 3–4 minutes. Serve with rice.

Lemon Pork and Rice Balls

o o o

○ Combine the minced pork, rice, onion, garlic and herbs in a large mixing bowl. Add the egg yolk and season with salt and freshly ground black pepper. Mix thoroughly to combine all the ingredients. Using slightly damp hands, shape the mixture into 5cm/2in balls and dredge with flour.

○ Place the olive oil in a large, deep frying pan with the meatballs. Add enough boiling water to just cover the meatballs. Cover and simmer for 35–40 minutes, or until the meat and rice are cooked, adding a little extra water to keep the meatballs covered during cooking if necessary.

○ To make the lemon sauce; beat together the eggs and lemon juice until frothy. Whisk in 2 tbsp of the cooking liquid from the meatballs, whisking vigorously to prevent curdling. Remove the frying pan from the heat and pour the egg mixture over the meatballs. Return the frying pan to the heat and stir continuously, until thickened. Do not allow the sauce to boil. Transfer the meatballs and sauce to a warm serving dish and garnish with chopped parsley.

*I*n Greece this dish is called "little spheres". It is a cross between a hearty soup and stew.

SERVES 8–10

450g/1lb minced pork
150g/5oz long-grain
* rice*
1 large onion, finely
* chopped*
2 garlic cloves, crushed
60ml/4 tbsp very finely
* chopped fresh*
* parsley*
30ml/2 tbsp chopped
* fresh mint*

5ml/1 tsp dried
* oregano*
1 egg yolk
salt and freshly ground
* black pepper, to taste*
flour, for dredging
45ml/3 tbsp olive oil
3 eggs, beaten
freshly squeezed juice
* of 2 lemons, strained*
chopped fresh parsley

Beef Koftas

○ ○ ○

SERVES 4

1 medium onion, peeled
  and finely chopped
1 clove garlic, crushed
450g/1lb lean minced
  beef
2.5cm/1in piece fresh
  root ginger, grated
salt and freshly ground
  pepper
2.5ml/½ tsp coriander,
  crushed or ground
5ml/1 tsp fresh
  breadcrumbs

15ml/1 tbsp yoghurt
5ml/1 tsp freshly
  chopped parsley
2.5ml/½ tsp lemon juice
225–275g/8–10oz rice
2.5ml/½ tsp turmeric
30ml/2 tbsp oil
30ml/2 tbsp chopped
  pineapple
25g/1oz flaked almonds

○ Sweat the onion and garlic in a little oil for about 4 minutes.

○ Mix the minced beef in a bowl with ginger, seasoning, coriander, breadcrumbs, yoghurt, parsley and lemon juice.

○ Add the onion mixture and mix thoroughly. Form into 8 sausage shapes.

○ Meanwhile put the long-grain rice on to cook with the turmeric and 1 teaspoon of salt for 15 minutes when all water should have been absorbed.

○ Place the minced beef mixture on wooden skewers. Brush with oil and brown under a hot grill turning every 2 minutes to cook and brown evenly.

○ Mix the rice with the pineapple and serve in a heated dish scattered with flaked almonds. Serve the koftas on top. Serve cucumber and pineapple yoghurt as a side dish or a barbecue or curry sauce.

Poultry Main Dishes

Braised Chicken in White Wine with Tomato and Rice Stuffing

○ ○ ○

*N*utty brown rice is used in the stuffing to make this a perfect dinner party recipe. Serve the sauce separately for those who want to control the flow of calories.

SERVES 6

125g/4oz cooked brown
  rice
75g/3oz garlic sausage,
  chopped
15ml/1 tbsp fresh
  parsley, chopped
3 tomatoes, skinned,
  deseeded and
  chopped
salt and freshly ground
  black pepper
2 egg yolks
1.5kg/3½lb oven-ready
  chicken
1 sweet red pepper

30ml/2 tbsp olive oil
1 shallot or small sweet
  onion, finely chopped
125g/4oz large cup
  mushrooms, thickly
  sliced
300ml/½pt chicken
  stock
10ml/2 tsp cornflour
45ml/3 tbsp single
  cream
10ml/2 tsp freshly
  chopped basil or
  2.5ml/½ tsp dried

○ Prepare the stuffing by mixing together the rice, garlic sausage, parsley, tomatoes and 1 egg yolk. Season with salt and pepper. Spoon inside the neck end of the chicken and fold the flap of skin over (securing with a small metal skewer if necessary).

○ Place the sweet red pepper under a hot grill, and turn until it is blistered all over. Put in a polythene bag and leave to "sweat" for 10 minutes. The skin can then easily be removed. Discard the seeds and thickly slice the flesh.

○ Heat the oil in a large flameproof casserole, add the chicken and cook over a moderate heat, turning until golden brown all over. Lift out and set aside; add the shallots or onion and mushrooms to the pan and cook for a few minutes until softened.

○ Return the chicken to the casserole, add the sliced sweet pepper and pour over the wine and stock. Cover and cook in the oven at 180°C/350°F/Gas 4 for 1 hour 20 minutes, or until tender.

○ Lift the chicken out onto a serving dish and remove the skewer if necessary. Using a slotted spoon, arrange the mushrooms and peppers around the chicken, and keep warm.

○ Stir the basil into the pan and simmer on the hob for 5 minutes. Beat the remaining egg yolk, cornflour and cream together and stir into the pan. Heat gently until the sauce thickens.

○ Joint or carve the chicken and accompany each serving with a spoonful of stuffing. Serve the sauce separately.

Gumbo

○ ○ ○

*G*umbo is a spicy stew of meat and vegetables served over rice. It comes from New Orleans, where cooks include all kinds of meats. This recipe calls for a combination of chicken, prawns and spicy smoked sausage.

SERVES 8

4 chicken breasts, skinned and cubed
30ml/2 tbsp flour
2.5ml/½ tsp salt
1.5ml/¼ tsp black pepper
1.5ml/¼ tsp cayenne pepper
5ml/1 tsp paprika
2.5ml/½ tsp onion powder
2.5ml/½ tsp garlic powder
30ml/2 tbsp oil
225g/8oz onion, chopped
125g/4oz green pepper, chopped
175g/6oz celery, chopped
2 cloves garlic, crushed

125g/4oz vegetable oil
50g/2oz flour
2l/3½pt chicken stock
3 medium tomatoes, seeded and chopped
350g/12oz Andouille sausage or other spicy smoked sausage, sliced
350g/12oz medium prawns, peeled and deveined
50g/2oz spring onions, chopped
15g/½oz fresh parsley, chopped
about 1kg/2lb cooked rice

○ Mix 30ml/2 tbsp flour with the salt and other seasonings. Sprinkle over the cubed chicken and toss so the cubes are evenly coated. Heat 30ml/2 tbsp oil in a frying pan and sauté the chicken until it is cooked through and lightly browned, 8–10 minutes. Refrigerate.

○ Have the chopped onion, pepper, celery and garlic ready before you make the roux. Heat the oil in a medium saucepan. The pan should be a little oversized for the quantity you're cooking because the roux gets dangerously hot, and you will want the extra depth in case it splashes around.

○ When the fat is hot, add the flour and whisk it in until the mixture is smooth. Turn the heat to low. Continue cooking, stirring constantly. The roux will turn ivory, then beige, then gradually darken through different shades of brown. Cook until the roux is darker than a golden-brown

bread crust, but has not turned chocolate brown. This will take about 30 minutes over low heat. You must stir constantly to keep the roux from burning. If black flecks appear in the roux, discard it and start again. The burned flavour will permeate the gumbo and ruin it. Never taste or touch the roux, and use extreme caution while stirring. Its temperature can reach 260°C/500°F.

○ When the roux reaches a medium brown, remove it from the heat. It will continue darkening, even away from the heat source. The way to stop the cooking is to add the chopped vegetables. Gradually and carefully stir in the vegetables until they are coated with roux. Then return

the roux to the cooker, and cook until vegetables are limp, about 5 minutes. Remove from heat.

○ In a large pan, bring 2l/3½pt of chicken stock to the boil. Add a few spoonfuls to the roux and stir, then add the roux to the stock. Add the cooked chicken, tomatoes and sausage. Simmer uncovered for 20 minutes, stirring occasionally. If the sausage is fatty, you may need to skim fat off the top of the gumbo. Taste and adjust seasonings.

○ Just before serving, add the prawns to the gumbo and cook until prawns turn white-pink and are tightly curled, 2–3 minutes. Stir in the spring onions and parsley, and serve in bowls over rice.

Cajun Duck Rice

○ ○ ○

*U*se leftover duck meat for this delicious, one-dish meal. If you have only a few scraps of duck left, add them to the rice and use it as a side dish instead of a main dish.

SERVES 4–6

30ml/2 tbsp duck fat or vegetable oil	*10ml/2 tsp fresh thyme or 2.5ml/½ tsp dried*
125g/4oz chopped onions	*10ml/2 tsp paprika*
50g/2oz sliced mushrooms	*2.5ml/½ tsp black pepper*
350g/12oz uncooked rice	*30ml/2 tbsp finely chopped celery leaves*
750ml/1¼pt duck stock	*125g/4oz chopped spring onions*
10ml/2 tsp salt	*350g/12oz cooked duck meat, cut into pieces*

○ In a frying pan over medium heat, heat the duck fat or oil. Sauté the onions and mushrooms until the onions are translucent, about 5 minutes. Add the rice and cook until it is lightly browned, about 5 minutes.

○ Meanwhile, in a saucepan, bring the duck stock, seasonings and celery leaves to the boil. Combine the rice and stock mixtures in a lightly greased 2l/3½pt casserole dish and stir in the duck and spring onions. Cover and bake at 180°C/350°F/Gas 4 until all the liquids are absorbed and rice is cooked, about 1 hour.

Yellow Chicken Curry

o o o

*A*n Indian-influenced curry dish very popular in Thailand.

SERVES 6

1.25l/2pt thin coconut milk
450g/1lb chicken, cut into medium-sized pieces

200g/7oz potatoes, peeled and cut into 1cm/½in cubes
10ml/2 tsp salt
45ml/3 tbsp sliced shallots, lightly fried

YELLOW CURRY PASTE

5 dried red chillies, chopped
10 small garlic cloves, chopped
½ stalk of lemon grass, sliced
8ml/½ tbsp sliced shallot
10ml/2 tsp curry powder

5ml/1 tsp sliced ginger
5ml/1 tsp sliced galangal
5ml/1 tsp shrimp paste
5ml/1 tsp salt
2.5ml/½ tsp coriander seeds
2.5ml/½ tsp fennel seeds

O Pound all the curry paste ingredients together with a pestle and mortar or in a blender to form a fine paste.

O Heat 250ml/8fl oz of the coconut milk in a wok or pan and cook the curry paste for 5 minutes. Add the rest of the coconut milk, bring to a boil, add the chicken and cook until tender, about 10 minutes.

O Add the potato and salt, and cook until the potatoes are done, about 10 minutes. Pour into soup bowls and sprinkle with the fried shallots.

O Serve accompanied by cucumber salad, sliced pickled ginger and rice.

Caribbean Chicken Pilau

o o o

SERVES 6

1 onion, chopped
2 garlic cloves
15ml/1 tbsp chopped fresh chives
15ml/1 tbsp chopped fresh thyme
2 celery sticks with leaves, chopped
60ml/4 tbsp water
fresh coconut meat from ½ coconut, chopped
liquid from fresh coconut
450g/1lb can pigeon peas, drained

1 fresh hot pepper
5ml/1 tsp salt
freshly ground black pepper
30ml/2 tbsp vegetable oil
30ml/2 tbsp sugar
1.5kg/3½lb chicken, chopped
225g/8oz uncooked rice, washed and drained
300ml/10fl oz water

O Grind the onion, garlic, chives, thyme, and celery with 4 tablespoons water in a blender or food processor. Empty the mixture into a large saucepan.

O Make coconut milk using the coconut meat and liquid.

O Add the coconut milk to the pan, together with the pigeon peas and hot pepper. Cook over a low heat for 15 minutes, then season with the salt and freshly ground black pepper to taste.

O Heat the oil in a flameproof casserole. Add the sugar and heat until it begins to caramelize.

O Add the raw chicken to the casserole, and cook for 15 minutes until it has browned. Stir in the pigeon pea mixture, rice and 300ml/10fl oz of water. Bring to the boil, reduce the heat, cover, and simmer for 20 minutes or until the rice and chicken are cooked. Discard the hot pepper before serving.

RIGHT **Caribbean Chicken Pilau**

Turkey Escalopes with White Wine and Mushrooms

○ ○ ○

This dish can also be made with veal escalopes.

SERVES 4

2 large turkey breasts, boned
15ml/1 tbsp flour
1.5ml/¼ tsp paprika
25g/1oz butter
30ml/2 tbsp vegetable oil

1 medium-sized onion, peeled
125g/4oz mushrooms, washed and sliced
30–45ml/2–3 tbsp white wine

SAUCE

300ml/½pt milk
1 slice of onion
1 bouquet garni
1 bay leaf
4 slightly crushed peppercorns

20g/¾oz butter
20g/¾oz flour
salt and pepper
225g/8oz savoury or plain boiled rice

○ Cut the turkey breasts in half and place the halves between a sheet of foil or cling film (plastic wrap) and beat out to an escalope shape with a rolling pin.

○ Mix the flour with the paprika and coat the turkey.

○ Heat the butter and oil in a frying pan and over medium to high heat fry on both sides until golden. They will need about 5 minutes each side. Keep warm in a low oven.

○ Cut one thick slice from the onion and cut the remainder into fine dice. Over a low heat cook the onion in the pan with oil from the turkey. After 3 minutes add the mushrooms and stir occasionally. Add the white wine and leave for 2 minutes over a very low heat.

○ Meanwhile put the milk with the slice of onion, bouquet garni, bay leaf and peppercorns on a low heat. Allow to come to almost boiling point. Then turn the heat off. Leave to infuse for 10 minutes covered.

○ Melt the butter in a small saucepan, add the flour and make a roux. Stir for 1 minute, then strain in the infused milk gradually to make a béchamel sauce. Cook until smooth. Add the onion and mushroom mixture and cook for a further 2–3 minutes.

○ Serve with savoury or plain boiled rice. Place the escalopes on the rice and pour the mushroom sauce over the escalopes and rice.

Spiced Chicken and Almond Rice

o o o

SERVES 4

350g/12oz chicken
  breasts
15ml/1 tbsp flour
2.5ml/½ tsp paprika
50g/2oz butter
50g/2oz slivered
  almonds
1 onion, peeled and
  finely chopped

30ml/2 tbsp vegetable
  oil
225g/8oz basmati rice
chicken stock
1cm/½in fresh root
  ginger, grated
15ml/1 tbsp soya sauce

O Cut the chicken breasts into strips about 0.5cm/⅛in.

O Mix the flour and paprika and coat each strip of chicken.

O Heat the butter over a medium heat and fry the almonds until golden on each sides. Remove to a plate with a spoon.

O Lower the heat and cook the onion until translucent for 3–4 minutes. Remove from the pan.

O Add the oil and, on a fairly high heat, cook the chicken strips for 5 minutes turning until golden on all sides. Remove from the pan.

O Wash the basmati rice thoroughly in about 5 changes of water. Drain well before adding to the frying pan. Gradually add the chicken stock, stirring with a fork. Cover and cook for 15 minutes.

O Remove the lid and stir in the onions, chicken and ginger. Gradually add the soya sauce and cook for 5 minutes.

O Sprinkle the dish with almonds and a little extra paprika. Decorate with a few petals of almonds.

Puerto Rican Chicken and Rice Stew

○ ○ ○

○ Mix the garlic, oregano, and salt together in a large bowl. Add the chicken pieces, and mix them well together. Heat the butter or margarine in a saucepan, and brown the chicken pieces. Transfer them to a plate.

○ Add the onion and green peppers to the pan, and cook until soft.

○ Add the tomatoes and browned chicken pieces, coating them well with the onion, peppers, and tomato mixture. Reduce the heat and simmer for 30 minutes, or until the chicken is cooked.

○ Remove the chicken to a plate and leave to cool a little.

○ Remove the bones, and cut the flesh into 5cm/2inch pieces.

○ Meanwhile, add the rice, stock and freshly ground black pepper to the onion, peppers and tomato mixture, and bring to the boil. Reduce the heat, cover, and simmer for 20 minutes or until the rice is cooked.

○ Stir in the peas, Parmesan, and hot pepper. Mix well, then add the chicken. Cover and simmer for 2 more minutes, then serve.

SERVES 6

1 garlic clove, chopped
2.5ml/½ tsp dried
   oregano
2.5ml/½ tsp salt
1.3kg/3lb chicken, cut
   into 8 pieces
50g/2oz butter or
   margarine
1 small onion, finely
   chopped
150g/5oz green
   peppers, chopped
4 ripe tomatoes,
   skinned and chopped

350g/12oz uncooked
   long-grain white rice
2.25l/3¾pt chicken
   stock
freshly ground black
   pepper
450g/1lb frozen peas
60ml/4tbsp Parmesan
   cheese, freshly grated
1 fresh hot pepper,
   chopped

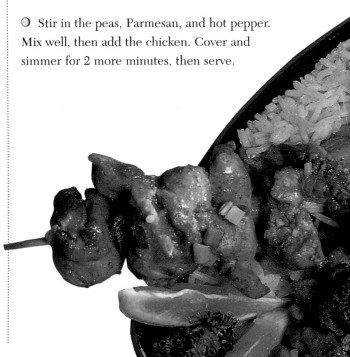

Chicken Saté

o o o

SERVES 4

650g/1½lb chicken without bone

MARINADE

*1 spring onion, washed
and chopped
2.5cm/1in fresh root
ginger, grated
grated rind of 1 lemon
1.5ml/¼ tsp ground
cinnamon*

*6 cardamom pods
5ml/1 tsp cumin
5ml/1 tsp ground
coriander
5ml/1 tsp peanut butter
150ml/¼pt coconut milk*

LEFT Chicken Saté

SAUCE

*90ml/6 tbsp peanut
butter
1 onion, peeled and
finely chopped
2 fresh chilli peppers,
seeded*

*1 clove garlic, crushed
juice of 1 lemon
30ml/2 tbsp chicken
stock or coconut milk*

GARNISH

1 spring onion, chopped

O Make up the marinade by mixing all the Marinade ingredients with the coconut milk.

O Cut the chicken into small pieces.

O Marinate the chicken overnight in the refrigerator or at least for several hours. Remove from the marinade and thread onto wooden or metal skewers.

O Mix all Sauce ingredients together and cook for 10 minutes. (The best sauce is made by blending all ingredients together.)

O Grill the chicken on skewers for 4 minutes each side under a high heat. Then allow to cook for a further 4 minutes each side under a medium heat.

O Serve with boiled rice or a rice salad. Garnish sauce with chopped spring onion.

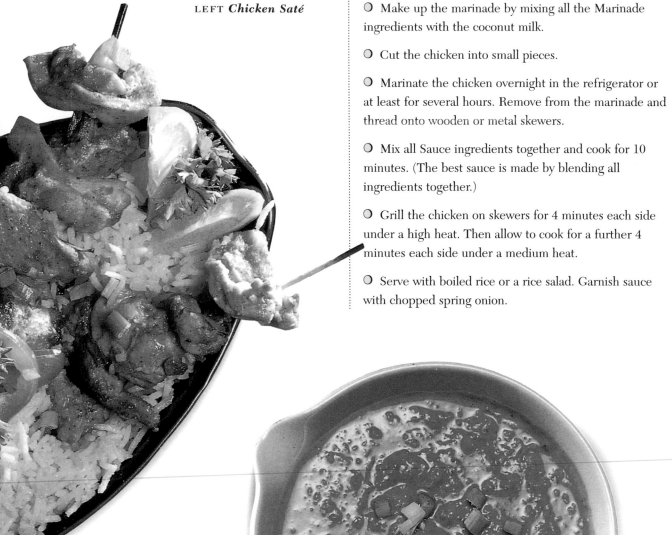

Portuguese Chicken with Rice

o   o   o

*T*he Arabs introduced rice-growing to Portugal and vibrant green paddy fields can still be seen in the lagoons along the west coast. Adding rice is a good way of making meat go further; in this recipe, the *chouriço* adds extra flavour.

SERVES 4

1 large onion, chopped
60ml/4 tbsp olive oil
2 garlic cloves, finely chopped
1–2 fresh red chillies, seeded and chopped
1 red pepper, cored, seeded and chopped
4 boneless chicken breasts, skinned and cut into thin strips
350g/12oz long-grain rice
600ml/1pt chicken stock

100ml/3½fl oz medium-bodied dry white wine, or additional stock
salt and pepper
225g/8oz chouriço (chorizo), cut into thick slices
125g/4oz frozen peas
10 oil-cured black olives, pitted and sliced
30ml/2 tbsp chopped parsley

○ Cook the onion in the oil in a large flameproof casserole until softened. Add the garlic, chillies, red pepper and chicken, and cook gently for 2–3 minutes.

○ Add the rice, stock, wine and seasoning. Bring to the boil, then cover and simmer for 12 minutes.

○ Stir in the *chouriço* (chorizo), peas, olives and parsley until just mixed, then cover the casserole and cook for a further 6 minutes or until the liquid has been absorbed and the rice is tender.

○ Fluff up with a fork and serve immediately.

Chicken, Andouille and Prawn Jambalaya

o o o

*A*ll the spiciness in this jambalaya comes from the meat. Be sure to taste before you serve, and adjust seasonings, especially if you've had to substitute other ham or sausage for the Tasso and Andouille. This level is hot and spicy to most people, but not as spicy as traditional Cajun cooking, so add more black and cayenne pepper if you like mouth-searing food.

SERVES 6–8

5ml/1 tsp salt

2.5ml/½ tsp cayenne

2.5ml/½ tsp black pepper

7.5ml/1½ tsp fresh or 2.5ml/½ tsp dried thyme

1 whole or 2 half uncooked chicken breasts, skinned and cubed

30ml/2 tbsp vegetable oil

3 stalks celery, chopped

2 medium onions, chopped

2 medium green peppers, chopped

2 garlic cloves, finely chopped

125g/4oz Tasso or other smoked ham, chopped

150g/5oz Andouille or other spicy sausage, sliced

450g/1lb tomatoes, seeded and chopped

225g/8oz can tomato sauce

250ml/8fl oz poultry or seafood stock

225g/8oz medium prawns, shelled and deveined

125g/4oz spring onions, chopped

600g/1¼lb cooked rice to serve

O In a small bowl, mix together the salt, cayenne, black pepper and thyme. Toss the chicken, until it is well coated with spices.

O In a large frying pan, heat the oil. Sauté the chicken, stirring almost constantly, until the chicken is browned, 6–8 minutes. Add the celery, onion, green pepper and garlic, and sauté until the vegetables are limp, about 5 minutes.

O Add the Tasso, Andouille sausage, tomatoes, tomato sauce and stock and stir and cook until mixture is bubbling. Reduce the heat and simmer until tomatoes have cooked down and liquid is slightly reduced, creating a rich, red broth. Add the prawns and cook until the prawns are opaque and tightly curled, 2–3 minutes. Taste and adjust the seasonings. It should be very spicy. Add the spring onions and enough rice so that the mixture is neither soupy nor dry.

O Note: if you did not cook the rice with salt, you will need to increase the amount of salt in the jambalaya.

Chicken Biriani

o o o

SERVES 4

225g/8oz long-grain
   rice, preferably
   basmati
15ml/1 tbsp salt
2 large onions, peeled
2 cloves garlic, crushed
2.5cm/1in piece root
   ginger, grated
90ml/6 tbsp vegetable
   oil
2–3 boned chicken
   portions
15ml/1 tbsp flour
1.5ml/¼ tsp chilli
   powder

5ml/1 tsp cumin,
   ground
75ml/5 tbsp yoghurt
15ml/1 tbsp lemon juice
60ml/4 tbsp water
5ml/1 tsp ground
   coriander
1.5ml/¼ tsp ground
   cinnamon
2.5ml/½ tsp turmeric
50g/2oz slivered
   almonds
onion rings
1 hard-boiled egg
1 tomato, skinned

○ Wash the rice several times. Allow to soak in a large bowl of water and salt for at least 1 hour.

○ Slice half an onion finely into rings and reserve. Place remaining onion, garlic, ginger, 1 tablespoon oil and some water in an electric grinder or food processor with a few slivered almonds. Grind to a paste.

○ Heat the remaining oil on a fairly high heat and fry onion rings until golden brown. Remove with a slotted spoon and drain on absorbent kitchen paper towels.

○ Fry the remaining slivered almonds until golden on each side and drain with the onion rings.

○ Cut the chicken into small pieces and toss in seasoned flour mixed with the chilli powder. Fry until golden and drain onto kitchen paper.

○ Fry the paste in fat. Add the yoghurt, 1 tablespoon at a time, with lemon juice. Add 4 tablespoons water and return the chicken to cook over a low heat for 15 minutes.

○ Add the coriander, cumin and cinnamon to the chicken after 5 minutes and stir well.

○ Meanwhile cook the rice in 1l/1¾pt boiling salted water with the turmeric for 10 minutes and drain.

○ Spread the drained rice on top of the chicken casserole. Add the almonds.

○ Cover the mixture with foil and then the casserole lid and bake in the oven for 35 minutes at 150°C/300°F/ Gas 2.

○ Mix the chicken and rice well with a fork and turn into heated serving dish. Garnish with sliced hard-boiled eggs and browned onion rings. Serve with accompaniments such as cucumber, mango chutney, poppadoms, chapatis or a vegetable curry.

Oriental Duck

o   o   o

SERVES 4

1 duck, approximately 2kg/4½lb	4 spring onions, washed and chopped

MARINADE

45ml/3 tbsp soya sauce	rind and juice of 1 lemon
30ml/2 tbsp honey	30ml/2 tbsp sherry
1cm/½in fresh root ginger, grated	30ml/2 tbsp vegetable oil

ACCOMPANIMENT

60ml/4 tbsp stock or water	225g/8oz bean shoots
200g/7oz water chestnuts	15ml/1 tbsp sherry and soya sauce (optional)
	225g/8oz boiled rice

GRAVY (OPTIONAL)

1 small onion	15ml/1 tbsp flour
salt and freshly ground pepper	

O Remove the giblets from the duck. Place the duck in a dish or plastic bag.

O Place half the spring onions in a bowl with the ingredients of the marinade. Mix and pour over the duck. Stand in the refrigerator. If you are using a plastic bag turn the duck from time to time. Otherwise baste the duck. Allow to marinate for several hours or overnight.

O Remove the duck from the marinade. Place it on a rack on top of a roasting pan. Put in the oven at 200°C/400°F/Gas 6 for 30 minutes to crisp.

O Turn down the heat to 180°C/350°F/Gas 4 and cook for a further 1¼ hours.

O Tip the remaining marinade into a saucepan and bring to the boil. Add the stock or water and simmer for 5 minutes. Then add the sliced water chestnuts, bean shoots, the remaining spring onions, and, if you wish, the sherry and soya sauce. The vegetables should be timed to be served with the cooked duck.

O The duck giblets may be boiled with water, onion and seasoning to make gravy. To do this, remove the duck from the oven and keep it warm. Pour off the excess fat, leaving the juices behind. Add the flour to the juices. Stir over a heated ring and season well. Add 150ml/¼pt giblet stock and whisk until a rich gravy is made. Pour over the carved duck, and accompany with the vegetables and rice.

Nasigoreng

○ ○ ○

*T*his dish originates from Malaysia, and makes good use of any left-over cooked meat, fish and vegetables. It is quick to prepare and makes the perfect informal fork supper dish.

SERVES 4–6

225g/8oz long-grain rice	*225g/8oz cooked*
60ml/4 tbsp groundnut	*chicken, diced*
oil	*75g/6oz cooked*
2 onions, finely chopped	*prawns, coarsely*
1 clove garlic, finely	*chopped*
chopped	*salt and freshly ground*
1 fresh red chilli, finely	*black pepper*
shredded	*30ml/2 tbsp chopped*
2 tomatoes, skinned,	*fresh coriander*
seeded and chopped	

OMELETTE

15ml/1 tbsp groundnut	*30ml/2 tbsp light soya*
oil	*sauce*
3 spring onions finely	*4 eggs, beaten*
chopped	*paprika*
salt and freshly ground	*cucumber slices*
black pepper	

○ Cook the rice until just tender. Drain thoroughly and spread out on a tray to cool.

○ Heat the oil in a large pan. Sauté the onions and garlic until softened and golden. Add the chilli and cook for a further 2 minutes.

○ Stir in the tomatoes, chicken and prawns. Cook for 2 minutes, then add the rice. Stir-fry until the rice turns a light golden colour. Season to taste. Stir in the fresh coriander.

○ Mound the rice mixture onto a platter, cover and keep warm.

○ For the omelette, heat the oil in a large frying pan. Add the spring onions and cook until softened.

○ Season with salt and pepper and add the soya sauce. Cook for a further 2 minutes.

○ Stir the beaten eggs into the pan. Cook over a low heat until the omelette is set.

○ Carefully remove the omelette from the pan onto a chopping board. Loosely roll and shred it finely.

○ Arrange the shreds of omelette over the rice. Sprinkle with a light dusting of paprika and garnish with cucumber slices. Serve immediately, with extra soya sauce and a selection of salads and relishes.

Chicken Risotto

○ ○ ○

A true Italian risotto uses Arborio rice, which contributes to the characteristic creamy texture. If you prefer a slightly "wetter" risotto, add a little more stock (or wine!).

SERVES 4–6

450g/1lb boneless chicken breast, skinned and cubed
30ml/2 tbsp sunflower oil
1 onion, finely sliced
2 cloves garlic, crushed
5ml/1 tsp dried oregano
225g/8oz Arborio or long grain rice
15ml/1 tbsp tomato purée

1.25/2pt strong chicken stock
splash dry white wine
salt and freshly ground black pepper
6 tomatoes, skinned, deseeded and chopped
10 pitted black olives, halved
15ml/1tbsp chopped parsley or basil
50g/2oz Parmesan cheese, grated

○ Heat the oil in a large pan, and cook the onion and garlic over a gentle heat until softened. Add the chicken and cook until golden brown.

○ Add the oregano and rice and cook for a further minute, stirring well. Blend in the tomato purée, stock and wine. Season to taste and stir well.

○ Cook over a gentle heat for 25 to 30 minutes or until all the liquid has been absorbed, but the rice still has a nutty bite to it.

○ Lightly fork in the tomatoes, olives and chopped parsley or basil. Heat through for a further 2 minutes. Serve, sprinkled with the Parmesan cheese.

Bokari Pilaf

○ ○ ○

SERVES 4

450g/1lb chicken livers
60ml/4 tbsp vegetable oil
2 onions, peeled and diced
1 clove garlic, crushed
2 carrots, scraped and grated
350g/12oz basmati or long-grain rice

salt and freshly ground pepper
2.5ml/½ tsp turmeric
600ml/1pt chicken stock
200g/7oz canned tomatoes or 3 tomatoes, skinned
30ml/2 tbsp parsley, chopped

○ Trim and dice chicken livers.

○ Heat the oil in a large pan and fry the livers until golden brown.

○ Add the onions, garlic and carrots to the chicken livers and turn with a spoon for about 2 minutes.

○ Add the washed rice, seasoning, turmeric and stock. Cover and cook for 20 minutes. Remove the lid and stir gently. Add the chopped tomatoes and cook for a further 5–10 minutes until the rice is tender.

○ Sprinkle with chopped parsley and turn into a heated serving dish.

LEFT *Chicken Risotto*   TOP RIGHT *Bokari Pilaf*

Spanish Rice with Chicken Livers

○ ○ ○

SERVES 4

225g/8oz long-grain rice
600ml/1pt stock or water
5ml/1 tsp salt
2.5m l/½ tsp turmeric
30ml/2 tbsp vegetable oil
125g/4oz chicken livers, trimmed and chopped
1 onion, peeled and finely chopped

6 tomatoes, peeled and chopped or
    425g/15oz canned peeled tomatoes
salt and freshly ground pepper
1.5ml/¼ tsp sugar
2 red peppers, seeded, chopped and blanched
125g/4oz packet thawed petits pois
125g/4oz cooked prawns

○ Cook the long-grain rice with boiling water or stock to which the salt and turmeric has been added. Cook by absorption method (see page 10).

○ Meanwhile heat the oil in a frying pan, and over a medium heat fry the chopped chicken livers until golden brown. Turn the heat down and add the onion. Cook, stirring well, for 4 minutes. Add the tomatoes, salt, pepper, sugar and chopped peppers. Stir gently.

○ Add the thawed peas and prawns. Heat through in the vegetable mixture and mix in the warmed rice.

○ Turn out into a dish and serve hot. A little butter may be added if you like.

Coriander Chicken with Pilau Rice

○ ○ ○

*F*resh coriander has a unique, pungent flavour.

SERVES 4

15ml/1 tbsp sunflower oil
8 chicken thighs
1 large onion, sliced
5ml/1 tsp paprika
5ml/1 tsp ground cumin
2.5ml/½ tsp dried thyme
freshly ground black pepper

300ml/½pt well flavoured chicken stock
25g/1oz pitted black olives
30ml/2 tbsp fresh coriander, finely chopped
squeeze lemon juice

PILAU RICE

30ml/2 tbsp vegetable oil
50g/2oz whole blanched almonds, toasted
1 small onion, finely diced

50g/2oz sultanas or raisins
350g/12oz long-grain rice
750ml/1¼pt boiling water
2.5ml/½ tsp salt

○ Heat the oil in a large pan and fry the chicken until an even, rich brown. Transfer to a plate.

○ Add the onion to the remaining oil and cook until softened and golden. Stir in the paprika, cumin and turmeric and cook for a further minute. Add the thyme, black pepper and stock and bring to the boil.

○ Return the chicken to the pan, skin side down. Cover and simmer for 1 to 1¼ hours or until the chicken is tender.

○ Remove the chicken with a slotted spoon to a heated serving dish and keep warm.

○ Reduce the sauce by rapidly boiling until it thickens. Stir in the olives, coriander and lemon juice. Season to taste and pour over the chicken.

○ for the rice, heat the oil in a large pan and cook the onion until softened but not coloured. Add the toasted almonds, sultanas and rice, and cook for a further minute, stirring thoroughly.

○ Add the boiling water and salt. Bring to the boil, then cover and reduce the heat to a simmer. Cook for 15 minutes, or until all the water has been absorbed and the rice is tender, but still firm. Fork the rice lightly and serve with the chicken.

Seafood Main Dishes

Prawn Fried Rice

o o o

SERVES 4–6

30ml/2 tbsp vegetable
  oil
450g/1lb prawns,
  peeled
1 spring onion,
  chopped
50g/2oz fresh button
  mushrooms
1 courgette, thinly
  sliced
½ carrot, thinly sliced
50g/2oz French beans,
  cut into 2.5cm/1in
  lengths

15ml/1 tbsp rice wine
  or dry sherry
5ml/1 tsp light soya
  sauce
freshly ground black
  pepper
salt
600g/1¼lb plain boiled
  rice
2 spring onions, neatly
  chopped into rounds

O Heat 8ml/½ tbsp oil in a wok and stir-fry the prawns
for 1 minute. Remove and set aside.

O Add the remaining oil and sweat the spring onion. Add
the mushrooms and the other vegetables and stir-fry for
2 minutes over a high heat.

O Put the prawns back into the wok with the vegetables
and add the rest of the ingredients except the rice,
continuing to stir all the while.

O Add the rice and stir-fry until the rice has changed
colour. Place in a large serving bowl and garnish with the
chopped spring onions.

Paella Valenciana

o o o

This great star turn of the Valencian coast has always been cooked outdoors. Preparing it takes all morning and it is cooked by the men, so the whole thing becomes a party. The ingredients for it are rather special. It originally included snails and still has three sorts of beans in Valencia. This is a more modest version, but it still needs good stock and a suitably shallow, wide 32–35cm/13–14in paella pan.

It speeds things up to prepare the base for the rice in the paella pan, and to use a second pan for frying the shellfish and chicken pieces.

SERVES 6

350g/12oz paella or
   risotto rice
60–75ml/4–5 tbsp olive
   oil
1 onion, chopped
2 garlic cloves, finely
   chopped
1.25l/2pt fish stock
225ml/7fl oz dry white
   wine
15 saffron strands
   soaked in 30ml/2 tbsp
   hot water, or saffron
   powder
225g/8oz raw prawns,
   peeled

salt and freshly ground
   black pepper
pinch of cayenne
   pepper
6 chicken thighs or 3
   legs, halved
225g/8oz mussels,
   cleaned
5ml/1 tsp paprika
125g/4oz cooked green
   beans or peas
200g/7oz canned red
   pimentos, drained
45ml/3 tbsp chopped
   fresh parsley

O Fry the onion in 2 tablespoons of oil in the paella pan (the rice pan), adding the garlic when it softens. Warm the stock and wine together, soaking the saffron in a cupful of it.

O Meanwhile, start a second frying pan, heating 2 tablespoons of oil. Fry the peeled prawns for 2 minutes (skip this if they are already boiled), then reserve.

O Rub salt, pepper and the cayenne pepper into the chicken pieces and fry for about 10 minutes on each side, adding more oil if needed.

O Wash the rice in a sieve and drain. Add the rice to the onion in the paella pan, stir for a couple of minutes and sprinkle with the paprika. Add the saffron liquid and ⅓ of the stock and bring back to the boil. Set the kitchen timer for 20–25 minutes. When the liquid has been absorbed, add another third of the stock and distribute the mussels, prawns, and beans or peas round the pan.

O When the liquid has nearly gone, add the remaining stock and give the mixture its last stir. Add the chicken pieces, bedding them into the liquid round the pan. Simmer on the lowest heat (best on a heat diffuser) for about 8–10 minutes. The liquid should all disappear by the time the timer rings. Check that the rice is cooked.

O Cut the pimentos into strips and lay these across the rice. Then turn off the heat and wrap the paella pan in newspaper or foil, to keep in the steam. Let it stand for 10 minutes. The flavours will blend and the last drop of liquid should disappear. Sprinkle with parsley and serve. Spaniards drink red wine with paella.

Prawn Creole

o o o

The liquid in this version of Prawn Creole is reduced until the sauce becomes quite thick and flavourful. The water chestnuts add a crunchy Oriental texture.

SERVES 4–6

30ml/2 tbsp vegetable
  oil
1 large onion, chopped
8 cloves garlic, minced
2 large celery sticks,
  finely chopped
4 medium tomatoes,
  chopped
2 medium green sweet
  peppers, chopped
30ml/2 tbsp tomato
  purée
5ml/1 tsp hot pepper or
  Tabasco sauce
½ tsp dried oregano
5ml/1 tsp dried thyme

10ml/2 tsp
  Worcestershire sauce
1.5l/2½pt chicken stock
650g/1½lb prawns,
  shelled and deveined
225g/8oz can sliced
  water chestnuts,
  drained and rinsed
8ml/½ tbsp lime juice
salt and freshly ground
  black pepper
650g/1½lb cooked white
  long-grain rice
15ml/1 tbsp minced
  coriander or parsley

O Heat the oil in a large saucepan, frying pan or wok. Add the onion, garlic, celery, tomatoes and peppers and fry over moderate heat until tender. Then add the tomato purée, hot pepper sauce, oregano and thyme and blend, stirring constantly, for about 2 minutes.

O Add the Worcestershire sauce and chicken stock and bring to the boil over medium-high heat until thickened, about 30 minutes.

O Add the prawns and water chestnuts and simmer, uncovered, until the prawns are opaque throughout, about 4 minutes.

O Remove from the heat and adjust the seasoning with more hot pepper sauce to taste, lime juice and salt and pepper.

O Serve over a scoop of rice on warm dishes and sprinkle the top with coriander or parsley. Serve immediately.

RIGHT **Salmon
Coulibiac**

Salmon Coulibiac

o   o   o

SERVES 4

450g/1lb fresh salmon
30ml/2 tbsp white wine
1 bay leaf
1 bouquet garni

150ml/¼pt water
freshly ground pepper
½ onion

FILLING

50g/2oz butter
1 onion, peeled and
   finely chopped
125g/4oz mushrooms,
   washed and sliced
225g/8oz cooked long-
   grain rice

15ml/1 tbsp chopped
   parsley
1.5ml/1/4 tsp chopped
   dill
salt and freshly ground
   pepper
2 hard-boiled eggs,
   shelled and chopped

PASTRY

450g/1lb frozen puff
   pastry, thawed

1 egg

O Place the salmon in a deep saucepan, preferably on a trivet. If this is not available, place the fish on a piece of double foil, with two ends reaching up the sides of the saucepan, as this will make it easy to remove.

O Place the white wine, bay leaf, bouquet garni, water, pepper and ½ onion in a saucepan and bring to the boil, simmer for 10 minutes.

O Pour the liquid over the salmon and bring to the boil again. Turn the heat low as the salmon must be allowed to poach very gently for 15 minutes. Allow less time if the fish is in steaks. The liquid should only move slightly in the saucepan. Allow to cool in the fish liquor.

O Remove the fish from the saucepan and take off the skin. Remove any bones, and flake.

O For the filling heat the butter in a frying pan and cook the onion over a low heat for 4 minutes. Push to one side of the pan.

O Add the mushrooms. Cook for 3 minutes. Add the rice, herbs and seasoning. Mix and allow to cool.

O Divide the pastry into 4 pieces. Roll out one piece of pastry on a work surface into a 20cm/8in square.

O Divide the rice mixture into 4 portions and the salmon into 4 equal servings. Put half the first rice portion in the centre of the rolled-out pastry and place 1 salmon portion on top. Finally cover the other half of the first rice portion. Damp the edges of the pastry with cold water and fold the corners to the centre. Pinch the edges together, enclosing the filling. Repeat for the other 3 pastry parcels.

O Flake and flute the edges of the pastry and decorate with pastry leaves. Rest in the refrigerator for 20 minutes. Glaze with beaten egg and cook in a pre-heated oven 220°C/425°F/Gas 7 for 30 minutes until golden brown.

O Serve accompanied with hollandaise sauce.

Cajun Seafood Gumbo with Okra

○ ○ ○

*O*kra is used as the thickener, so this mildly spicy gumbo is lighter than a roux-based gumbo. Use at least three different types of fish and shellfish.

SERVES 8

30ml/2 tbsp vegetable oil
450g/1lb onions, chopped
2 large green peppers, chopped
2 stalks celery, chopped
3 garlic cloves, finely chopped
3 large or 4 medium tomatoes, seeded and chopped
225g/8oz tin tomato sauce
1.75l/3pt seafood stock
15ml/1 tbsp fresh-squeezed lemon juice

2 bay leaves
15ml/1 tbsp fresh thyme or 5ml/1 tsp dried
5ml/1 tsp salt
1.5ml/¼ tsp black pepper
large pinch cayenne
large pinch white pepper
2.5ml/½ tsp paprika
675g/1½lb okra, thawed and well drained if frozen, sliced
1kg/2lb mixed seafood
450g/1lb cooked rice to serve
filé powder (optional)

○ In a large frying pan, heat the oil. Sauté the onion, pepper, celery and garlic until limp, about 5 minutes. Transfer to a large saucepan or stockpot and add the tomatoes, tomato sauce, seafood stock, lemon juice and seasonings. Bring to the boil, then reduce the heat and simmer, uncovered, 5 minutes.

○ Add the okra and return to the boil, then reduce the heat and simmer 30 minutes. Add the seafood: cubed fish and frogs' legs take the longest times to cook, oysters the least.

○ Spoon the rice into individual large bowls. Ladle the gumbo over the rice. If desired, add a pinch of filé powder to each bowl.

Tuna and Rice Stuffed Peppers

o o o

SERVES 4

4 red or green peppers
175g/6oz long-grain
  rice
a pinch of saffron
  powder or turmeric
25g/1oz butter
1 onion, chopped
1 clove garlic, crushed
125g/4oz mushrooms,
  thinly sliced and
  blanched

175g/6oz can tuna fish,
  drained or 125g/4oz
  peeled prawns,
  chopped
15ml/1 tbsp chopped
  parsley
salt and freshly ground
  pepper
300ml/½pt Spicy
  Tomato Sauce (see
  page 63)

○ Blanch the whole peppers in salted water. Drain. Cut off the tops and scoop out the seeds.

○ Cook the rice with a pinch of saffron or turmeric in boiling salted water for 15 minutes until just cooked.

○ Strain and rinse in cold water. Drain well.

○ Melt the butter and soften the onion and garlic. Add the mushrooms, tuna, rice and parsley. Mix well and season to taste.

○ Spoon into the peppers and place in a well-greased dish. Cover with buttered paper or foil. Surround with the tomato sauce and bake in a moderate oven 180°C/350°F/Gas 4 for 30 minutes.

○ Sprinkle with any extra parsley.

Grilled Dublin Bay Prawns with Rice and Tomato Sauce

o o o

The fishing port of Peniche, on the coast of Portugal above Lisbon, is famed for its shellfish, particularly spiny lobster, Dublin Bay prawns (also known as scampi) and large prawns, which could also be used for this recipe.

SERVES 4

1 onion, finely chopped
350g/12oz long-grain
    rice
40g/1½oz butter
650g/1½lb raw Dublin
    Bay prawns or large
    prawns in their shells

olive oil for brushing
salt and pepper
about 30–45ml/2–3
    tbsp chopped parsley

SAUCE

1 onion, chopped
1 garlic clove, chopped
23ml/1½ tbsp oil
600g/1¼lb well-
    flavoured tomatoes,
    seeded and chopped

1 bouquet garni
150ml/¼pt medium-
    bodied dry white
    wine
12 oil-cured pitted
    black olives

○ To make the sauce, cook the onion and garlic in the oil until softened but not coloured. Stir in the tomatoes and cook for a few minutes before adding the bouquet garni, wine and olives. Simmer gently until it has thickened.

○ Meanwhile, cook the onion and rice in the butter, stirring, until golden. Add water to cover generously and bring to the boil. Then cover the pan and simmer for about 12 minutes until tender.

○ Preheat the grill. Thread the prawns on skewers, brush with oil and grill for 7–8 minutes, turning occasionally.

○ Drain the rice, rinse quickly with boiling water and stir in the parsley and seasoning.

○ Season the sauce and discard the bouquet garni. Serve the prawns on a bed of rice, accompanied by the sauce.

Curried Halibut Fillets

○ ○ ○

This dish comes from one of the Jewish communities in India, the southern city of Cochin. Cochin is near the Kerala Coast which produces fresh fish and is also famous for its spice market.

SERVES 6

15ml/1 tbsp vegetable oil
1 onion, cut in half and thinly sliced
2 to 3 garlic cloves, peeled and finely chopped
1kg/2lb halibut fillets, cut in 7.5cm/3in pieces
40g/1½oz fresh coriander leaves, chopped

15ml/1 tbsp red-wine vinegar
60ml/4 tbsp tomato purée
5ml/1 tsp ground cumin
2.5ml/½ tsp turmeric
1 small fresh red chilli, or 2.5ml/½ tsp red-pepper flakes
hot boiled rice for serving

○ In a large frying pan, over medium-high heat, heat oil. Add sliced onion and cook until softened and beginning to colour, 3–5 minutes. Add garlic and cook 1 minute longer.

○ Add fish and cook until the fish begins to firm and turn opaque, 4–5 minutes. Gently stir in remaining ingredients, except garnish and rice, and 125ml/4fl oz water and simmer 15 minutes, covered. The fish will flake easily if tested with the tip of the knife.

○ Remove fish fillets to a serving dish. Increase heat to high and cook sauce until slightly thickened, 2–3 minutes. Pour over fish fillets. Garnish with coriander sprigs and serve with hot rice.

Caribbean Prawn and Tomato Rice

○ ○ ○

SERVES 4

30ml/2 tbsp olive oil
1 garlic clove, crushed
2 tomatoes, peeled and
    chopped
5ml/1 tsp saffron
10ml/2 tsp salt
5ml/1 tsp paprika
350g/12oz peas
350g/12oz uncooked
    rice

freshly ground black
    pepper
600ml/1pt water
8 small prawns,
    cooked, shelled and
    deveined
12 scampi, cooked,
    shelled and deveined

○ Heat the oil in a saucepan, then fry the garlic in it for 2 minutes.

○ Add the tomatoes, saffron, salt, paprika, peas, rice, and freshly ground black pepper and fry for 5 minutes, then add the water.

○ Add the prawns and scampi and cook for 15 more minutes, or until the rice has cooked (if necessary adding some more water). Serve immediately.

○ Serve with a cucumber salad.

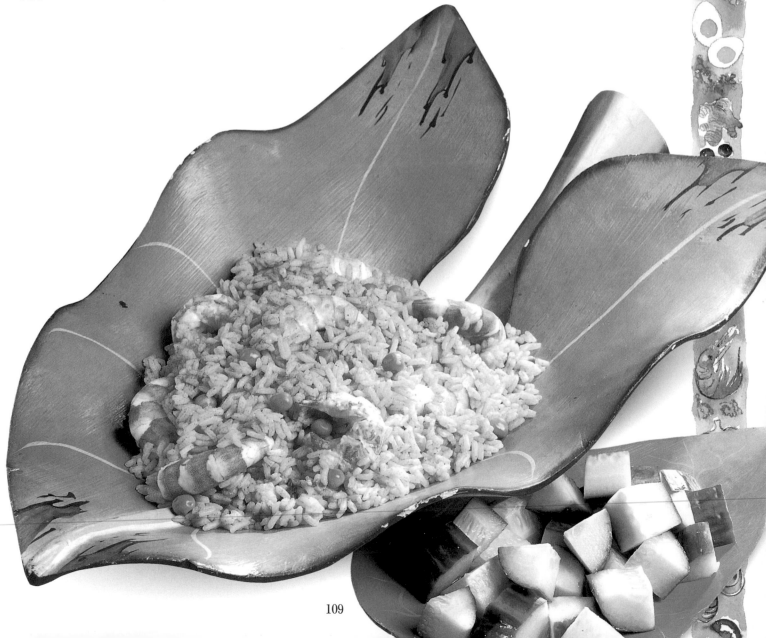

Crab Pilau

o o o

This recipe for rice with crab and coconut milk originated in Tobago.

SERVES 6

30ml/2 tbsp butter or
   margarine
30ml/2 tbsp vegetable
   oil
1 medium onion,
   chopped
1 garlic clove, chopped
2.5ml/½ tsp hot pepper,
   chopped
25ml/5 tsp curry
   powder

450g/1lb uncooked
   long-grain white rice,
   washed
900ml/1½pt coconut
   milk
5ml/1 tsp salt
freshly ground black
   pepper
450g/1lb fresh, canned,
   or frozen crabmeat
15ml/1 tbsp fresh lime
30ml/2 tbsp raisins

○ Melt the butter or margarine in a large saucepan over a medium heat. Add the oil, onion, garlic and hot pepper, and cook for 5 more minutes.

○ Add the curry powder and stir in, then add the rice and cook for 3 minutes.

○ Add the coconut milk, salt, and freshly ground black pepper to taste and bring to the boil over a high heat, then reduce the heat, cover, and simmer for 15 minutes.

○ Add the crabmeat and lime or lemon juice and simmer for 5 more minutes or until the liquid has been absorbed. Decorate with the raisins and serve hot.

○ Serve with a cucumber salad.

Seafood Jambalaya

o o o

Jambalaya is traditionally made with ham, but it's not a necessity. You may add ham, if you desire – 125–225g/4–8oz chopped ham – and if you use Tasso ham, you may need to decrease the seasonings.

SERVES 6–8

30ml/2 tbsp vegetable
   oil
1 onion, chopped
1 green pepper,
   chopped
2 stalks celery, chopped
3 cloves garlic, finely
   chopped
3 large tomatoes,
   seeded and chopped
250ml/8fl oz can
   tomato sauce
250ml/8fl oz seafood
   stock
50g/2oz chopped fresh
   parsley
2 bay leaves

15ml/1 tbsp fresh
   thyme or 5ml/1 tsp
   dried
5ml/1 tsp salt
1.5ml/¼ tsp black
   pepper
2.5ml/½ tsp cayenne
large pinch white
   pepper
1kg/2lb fresh prawns,
   crab meat, crawfish
   or oysters, or any
   combination,
   prepared
125g/4oz spring onions,
   chopped
450g/1lb cooked rice to
   serve

○ Heat the oil in a deep frying pan. Sauté the onion, green pepper, celery and garlic for about 5 minutes. Add the tomatoes, tomato sauce, stock, parsley and seasonings and simmer until the tomatoes are cooked down and the liquids reduced. Taste and adjust seasonings.

○ Add the seafood. (If using oysters, cut into bite-sized pieces and add in last 2–3 minutes of cooking.) Simmer just until the prawns are opaque and tightly curled, 5–7 minutes. Just before serving, mix in the spring onions. Serve over rice.

RIGHT **Seafood Jambalaya**

Kedgeree

o o o

This makes an excellent breakfast dish for guests as it can be prepared in advance and heated through just before serving.

SERVES 4

125g/4oz long-grain rice
3 hard-boiled eggs, shelled
salt and freshly ground pepper
225g/8oz smoked haddock

150ml/¼pt milk
1 bay leaf
1 slice of peeled onion
15ml/1 tbsp chopped parsley
2.5ml/½ tsp paprika
1 lemon, quartered

O Cook the rice by the absorption method (see page 10).

O Chop 2 hard-boiled eggs. Sieve the white and yolk of the third egg separately to garnish the kedgeree.

O Add the chopped eggs to the rice, with salt and pepper.

O Place the smoked haddock in a saucepan with the milk, bay leaf, onion and a little pepper. Bring to the boil and allow to simmer for 5 minutes. Allow to cool slightly in the milk. Remove and flake the fish from the skin. Add to the rice.

O Heat all the ingredients together and pile onto a heated serving dish.

O Garnish with rows of egg yolk, egg white and chopped parsley with a little paprika. Serve with lemon quarters.

Scandinavian Curried Cod

o o o

This curry sauce is equally good with chicken. Fried almonds add a delicious touch. Lettuce dressed with lemon vinaigrette is a good accompaniment.

SERVES 4–6

300ml/½pt water
225ml/7fl oz dry white wine
1 small leek or onion, sliced
5 white peppercorns

7.5ml/1½ tsp salt
450–600g/1–1¼lb cod fillets
boiled long-grain rice
almonds or salted peanuts fried in oil

CURRY SAUCE

25g/1oz butter
7.5ml/1½ tsp curry powder
30ml/2 tbsp plain flour
300ml/½pt strained fish stock

1 egg yolk
125–225ml/4–7fl oz cream
salt and pepper

O Mix the water, wine, leek or onion, peppercorns and salt in a pan. Bring to the boil, cover and simmer for 10 minutes.

O Rinse the fish fillets, fold them double and place in a wide saucepan. Strain the liquid and pour onto the fish. Simmer for 6–8 minutes.

O For the sauce, melt the butter, add the curry powder and flour, and heat without browning. Add the fish stock gradually, stirring, and simmer for a few minutes. Remove from the heat and whisk in the egg yolk with the cream. Season.

O Place the fish on a bed of boiled rice and pour over some of the sauce. Serve the rest separately. Garnish with fried almonds or salted peanuts.

Salmon with Dill and Ginger Vinaigrette

o   o   o

This recipe uses a cold water fish but gives it a Caribbean spice treatment. Serve with a Creole rice-and-beans dish (see page 24).

SERVES 4

4 x 175g/6oz boneless
   salmon fillets with
   skin on
9 large sprigs fresh dill
1 bay leaf
4 whole cloves

salt
9 whole black
   peppercorns
30ml/2 tbsp white wine
   vinegar

DILL AND GINGER VINAIGRETTE

30ml/2 tbsp French
   mustard
15ml/1 tbsp grated root
   ginger
30ml/2 tbsp finely
   chopped shallot
15ml/1 tsp finely
   chopped garlic

30ml/2 tbsp tarragon
   vinegar
50g/2oz canned
   pimentoes, diced
salt and freshly ground
   black pepper
100ml/3.5fl oz olive oil

◯ Prepare the vinaigrette by whisking the mustard, ginger, shallot, garlic, vinegar, pimentoes and salt and pepper together in a bowl. Then add the olive oil in a slow stream, whisking rapidly until well blended. Set aside.

◯ Place the salmon fillets in a shallow saucepan with enough water to cover. Add all but one dill sprig, the bay leaf, cloves, salt, peppercorns and vinegar. Bring the water to the boil and simmer for 3–5 minutes. Do not overcook. Drain and serve with the vinaigrette, giving the vinaigrette a last-second whisking, if necessary. Float the reserved sprig of dill on top of the bowl of vinaigrette.

Puddings

Rice Meringue

∘ ∘ ∘

SERVES 4

50g/2oz short-grain rice	25g/1oz sugar
7g/¼oz butter	2 eggs, separated
600ml/1pt milk	30ml/2 tbsp raspberry jam
rind of 1 lemon	50g/4oz sugar

○ Wash the rice several times in a sieve under the cold tap. Drain.

○ Butter an ovenproof dish and sprinkle the rice into the dish. Cover with the milk, lemon rind and sugar. Stir well.

○ Cook in the oven at 150°C/300°F/Gas 2 for 30 minutes. Remove, add the egg yolks and stir well. Continue cooking for a further 1 hour covered with foil.

○ Remove from the oven and spread the surface with jam. Allow to cool slightly.

○ Whisk the egg whites until light and fluffy. Add half the sugar and continue whisking until the mixture is glossy. Fold in the remaining sugar keeping back ½ teaspoon to sprinkle on top.

○ Pile the meringue mixture on top of the pudding and sprinkle with sugar. Return to the oven at the higher temperature of 180°C/350°F/Gas 4, and bake for 25 minutes when the topping will be golden and crisp on top.

Cajun Rice Pudding

∘ ∘ ∘

*R*ice pudding is a great way to use leftover rice. You may find yourself intentionally making too much rice for dinner, just so you have an excuse to make this old-fashioned custardy dessert.

SERVES 6

350ml/1fl oz milk	2.5ml/½ tsp cinnamon
25g/1oz butter, melted	1.5ml/¼ tsp grated nutmeg
4 eggs, lightly beaten	75g/3oz raisins
75g/3oz sugar	225g/8oz cooked rice
5ml/1 tsp vanilla essence	
5ml/1 tsp grated lemon peel	

○ In a large bowl, mix all the ingredients together, except the rice: spices have a tendency to clump, so use a wire whisk. Stir in the rice.

○ Pour into a buttered casserole dish (this will come right to the top of a 1.25l/2pt dish) and bake at 160°C/325°F/Gas 3, until the custard sets, about 1 hour, stirring once after about 15 minutes. Serve warm.

Calas

These sweet rice cakes are deep-fried, sprinkled with powdered icing sugar, and served for breakfast like small pastries. They are delicious hot, and it's hard to stop with just one or two.

MAKES ABOUT 20

2 eggs
75ml/5 tbsp sugar
10ml/2 tsp vanilla
* essence*
2.5ml/½ tsp grated
* nutmeg*
2.5ml/½ tsp grated
* lemon peel*

2.5ml/½ tsp salt
10ml/2 tsp baking
* powder*
225g/8oz cold cooked
* rice*
125g/4oz plain flour
vegetable oil for frying
powdered icing sugar

○ In a mixing bowl, combine the eggs and sugar and beat until pale yellow. Add the vanilla essence, nutmeg, lemon, salt, baking powder and rice, and mix well. Add enough flour to bind the ingredients.

○ In a deep frying pan or wok heat 7.5cm/3in oil to 185°C/365°F. (Remember that when oil gets above 180°C/350°F, the temperature can shoot up rapidly.) Drop teaspoonfuls of the batter into the oil, but do not crowd.

○ Fry until golden, turning once, about 4 minutes. Remove, drain briefly, place on absorbent paper towel and keep warm. Make sure the oil returns to 185°C/365°F before frying the next batch.

○ Sift powdered icing sugar over the calas, or put the sugar in a bag, add a few calas at a time, and shake.

Scandinavian Rice and Almond Pudding

In the early 1800s rice was imported so it was very expensive and reserved for special occasions only. Served hot or cold, tradition demands that a bowl is put out for Father Christmas on Christmas Eve.

SERVES 8–10

900ml/1½pt milk
50g/2oz caster sugar
200g/7oz long-grain
* white rice*
50g/2oz blanched
* almonds, halved*

1 small wine glass of
* sherry*
5–10ml/1–2 tsp vanilla
* essence*
225ml/7fl oz double
* cream, chilled*

○ Bring the milk to the boil. Add the sugar and rice, stirring occasionally. Lower the heat and simmer, uncovered, for about 25 minutes or until the rice is cooked. (To test, run a grain of rice between your thumb and forefinger, if there is no hard kernel in the centre then the rice is done.) Pour the rice immediately into a shallow bowl to cool it quickly.

○ When cool, add the almonds, sherry and vanilla essence. Whip the cream in a chilled bowl until it thickens and holds it shape. Fold in the rice mixture. Turn the pudding into a serving dish and chill. A cold sherry or raspberry sauce is often served on top.

RIGHT **Calas**

116

Rice Soufflé Pudding

SERVES 4–6

*125g/4oz short-grain
   rice*
75g/3oz sugar
50g/2oz butter
900ml/1½pt milk

4 eggs, separated
*1 vanilla pod or a few
   drops of vanilla
   essence*

SAUCE

*300ml/½pt blended
   pineapple*

10ml/2 tsp cornflour
30ml/2 tbsp water

○ Rinse the rice well several times in cold water and allow to drain in the sieve.

○ Sprinkle the rice into a pan of hot water. Bring to the boil and cook for 3 minutes. Drain and pour boiling water from the kettle over the grains.

○ Add the sugar and half the butter to most of the milk, keeping some to mix with the egg yolks. Add the vanilla pod at this stage but if you are using vanilla essence add it at the end of the cooking. Heat the mixture and add the rice. Cook until tender for about 30 minutes. After 15 minutes add a little of the hot rice to the egg yolks and milk and then return to the rice. Stir well for the remainder of the cooking time. Allow to cool slightly.

○ Butter a 18cm/7in soufflé dish. Pre-heat the oven. Put 1cm/½in water in the bottom of a roasting pan.

○ Whip up the egg whites to a fluffy consistency but do not over-beat. Fold the vanilla essence and egg whites in the rice mixture and turn into a soufflé dish standing in the water. Cook at 190°C/375°F/Gas 5 for 25–30 minutes.

○ For a sauce any blended fruit or fruit juice will do. Mix the cornflour with the water and add to the blended fruit. Heat over a low heat until slightly thickened.

○ This soufflé should be served straight from the oven.

Creamy Chilled Rice

○ ○ ○

*T*his dessert is served in the deep south of Spain for spoiling invalids and children and it was taken to Paris by Eugenia de Montijo, to become *riz à l'impératrice*. It is normally dusted with cinnamon, but can be decorated with mandarin segments or grapes.

SERVES 6

75g/3oz short-grain	*6 egg yolks*
rice	*powdered cinnamon*
1.25l/2pt milk	*2 lemons*
vanilla pod, split in 2	*225ml/7fl oz double or*
250g/9oz caster sugar	*whipping cream*

○ Wash the rice in a sieve under running water. Tip it into a pan of boiling water and cook for 5 minutes, then drain well.

○ Heat 450ml/15fl oz of milk in a pan and add the rice, half the vanilla pod and 4 tablespoons of sugar. Simmer until the rice has expanded and the mixture is thick (25 minutes or so). Cream the egg yolks with the remaining sugar in a heatproof bowl that fits over a pan of simmering water. Heat the remaining milk and pour it into the egg and sugar mixture, adding the rest of the vanilla pod. Cook gently, stirring, until the custard coats the back of a spoon. Remove the vanilla pod. Stir the rice into the custard with a pinch of cinnamon and leave until cold.

○ Cut 6 round discs of peel from the side of the lemons. Blanch them in boiling water for 2 minutes, then drain and refresh them under the cold tap. Whip the cream and fold into the rice. Turn into a shallow bowl and push the lemon peel into the rice at regular intervals. Chill well. Before serving, dust cinnamon over the top.

Imperial Rice Mould with Kiwi Fruit

○ ○ ○

SERVES 6

75g/3oz short-grain
    rice
75g/3oz sugar
75g/3oz candied fruit
600ml/1pt milk
3 egg yolks
15g/½oz gelatine
30ml/2 tbsp water

300ml/½pt whipping
    cream
10ml/2 tsp Kirsch
a few drops of vanilla
50g/2oz redcurrant
    jelly
2 kiwi fruit, peeled and
    sliced

○ Wash the rice and drain. Mix with the sugar and candied fruit in a saucepan. Pour in 450ml/¾pt milk and allow to stand for at least 30 minutes.

○ Mix the egg yolks with the remaining milk.

○ Cook the rice in a saucepan, uncovered, by bringing the milk almost to the boil and then stirring over a low heat for about 15 minutes or until the rice is tender. Add the egg yolks and milk for the last few minutes of cooking. Allow to cool.

○ Make up the gelatine by sprinkling it into 2 tablespoons of boiling water. It should dissolve but if the water has cooled too much stand the heatproof container in boiling water for a few minutes to make sure.

○ Whip the cream lightly. Flavour with the Kirsch.

○ Wet a mould. Place in the refrigerator to chill.

○ Stir the gelatine into the cooled rice with the vanilla and lastly fold in the whipped cream. Pour into the mould and leave to set.

○ Warm the redcurrant jelly. Unmould the rice onto a serving plate and run the slightly warmed jelly over the top.

○ Decorate with fruit.

Pineapple Fruit Flan

o o o

SERVES 4

SHORT CRUST PASTRY

175g/6oz plain flour	*35g/1¼oz white fat*
a pinch of salt	*1 egg, separated*
50g/2oz hard	*30–45ml/2–3 tbsp*
margarine or butter	*water*

FILLING

25g/1oz ground rice	*2.5ml/½ tsp cinnamon*
300ml/½pt milk	*1 egg yolk*
25g/1oz butter	*2 egg whites*
grated rind of 1 lemon	*15ml/1 tbsp sherry*
juice of ½ lemon	*275g/10oz pineapple*
5ml/1 tsp sugar	*pieces*

DECORATION

6 pieces of pineapple	*6 glacé cherries*

O To make the pastry, sieve the flour into a bowl and cut the fat into small nut-sized pieces. Rub the fat in with the tips of the fingers. Mix with egg yolk and add a little water, using a round-bladed knife until a smooth consistency is obtained. Tip onto a lightly-floured board and knead lightly until smooth. Place in a refrigerator for at least 15 minutes.

O Roll the pastry into a round about 3.5cm/1½in larger than the flan ring. Lift the pastry on a rolling pin and ease gently into the ring without stretching. Roll the top with the rolling pin and prick the bottom. Bake and cover with a piece of greaseproof paper weighted with baking beans for 15 minutes at 200°C/400°F/Gas 6.

O Meanwhile make up the sauce for the filling by whisking the ground rice, milk, butter, grated lemon rind, a few drops of juice, sugar and cinnamon over a low heat until thick. Allow to cool.

O When the mixture is fairly cool beat in the egg yolk and sherry.

O Chop or purée the fruit and line the bottom of the flan ring.

O Whisk the egg whites until fluffy but do not overbeat and fold into the rice mixture with a metal spoon. Tip into the flan ring and decorate with pieces of pineapple and cherries.

O Bake in the oven at 180°C/350°F/Gas 4 for 25 minutes.

121

Thai Sticky Rice with Mangoes

○ ○ ○

A simple dessert, but always successful. It works because of contrasts: in flavour between the sweetness of the coconut milk and the yellow Thai mango, and in texture between the rice and the mango.

SERVES 4–6

450g/1lb rice
775ml/28fl oz thin
   coconut milk
50g/2oz sugar

2.5ml/½ tsp salt
2.5ml/½ tsp cornflour
2 ripe mangoes, peeled
   and sliced

○ Soak the rice in water for 4 hours, rinse well 3 times in lukewarm water and drain very well. Line a strainer with cheesecloth, add the rice and place over a pan of boiling water – don't let the water touch the bottom of the rice. Cover and steam for about 30 minutes until fairly soft.

○ Mix 675ml/24fl oz of the coconut milk with the sugar and ¼tsp of the salt. Stir in the rice and mix well.

○ Mix the remaining coconut milk with the ¼ tsp salt and the cornflour together in a small pan, bring to a boil, simmer for 2 minutes and cool.

○ Place the sticky rice onto serving plates, spoon the cornflour sauce over the top and arrange the mango slices around the edges.

Sweet Egg Cream

○ ○ ○

*T*his sweet egg cream is used as part of a number of Portuguese desserts and sweets, or may be served in small portions for a dessert. At Aveiro, on the Beira Litoral coast, it is traditionally sold in small wooden barrels or white shell-shaped containers. The use of the water from cooking rice is a fairly recent practice but it improves the texture of the cream. The cream can be kept for 2–3 weeks in a covered container in the refrigerator.

SERVES 4–6

50g/2oz short-grain
   rice
450ml/¾pt water

225g/8oz sugar
8 large egg yolks

○ Simmer the rice in the water in a covered saucepan for about 30 minutes until tender. Strain and reserve 125ml/4fl oz of the water. Discard the rice or use it for another dish.

○ Heat the sugar gently in the reserved rice water, stirring constantly, until the sugar has dissolved. Boil until reduced to a light syrup.

○ Cool slightly and then pour on to the egg yolks slowly, whisking. Pour back into the pan in which the syrup was made and heat very gently, stirring, until thickened; do not allow it to boil as it will curdle.

○ Use as required, or pour into a dish or individual dishes and leave to cool.

Apricot Rice Mould

o o o

SERVES 4–6

125g/4oz short-grain
rice
125g/4oz sugar
75g/3oz butter
900ml/1½pt milk
4 eggs, separated

1 vanilla pod or a few
drops of vanilla
essence
150ml/¼pt whipping
cream
15g/½oz gelatine
425g/15oz canned
apricots

○ Wash the rice several times in a sieve and drain.

○ Add the sugar and butter to most of the milk in a saucepan. Retain 150ml/¼pt milk to mix with the egg yolks. Heat the milk, vanilla pod, butter and sugar. If using vanilla essence add at the end of cooking.

○ Sprinkle the rice into the milk mixture and stir over a low heat until the rice is cooked. Add a little of the hot rice mixture to the egg yolks and milk and return to the saucepan for the last 5 minutes of cooking time. Allow to cool.

○ Whip the cream lightly.

○ Make up the gelatine by sprinkling it into 150ml/¼pt hot apricot juice in a heatproof cup. Stand the cup in boiling water and stir to completely dissolve the gelatine.

○ Chop or blend half the apricot halves. Stir into the rice mixture with the gelatine. Allow to stand for 10 minutes.

○ Whisk the egg whites until light and fluffy, but not to the cotton wool (hard peak) stage.

○ Fold the cream and vanilla essence into the rice mixture and lastly fold in the egg whites. Turn into a large mould or cake pan and allow to set.

○ Decorate with the remaining apricots.

Rice Eggs with Peach Sauce

SERVES 4

75g/3oz short-grain
  rice
50g/2oz sugar
3 egg yolks
300ml/½pt milk

2.5ml/½tsp vanilla
  essence
15ml/1 tbsp sultanas
15ml/1 tbsp mixed
  nuts, chopped

TO COAT

1 egg
125g/4oz dried
  breadcrumbs

TO FRY

1l/1¾pt vegetable oil

PEACH SAUCE

1 small can of peaches

10ml/2 tsp arrowroot

O Wash the rice several times in cold water. Boil in a pan of water for 10 minutes. Drain into a sieve.

O Cook the rice and milk in a saucepan until the rice is soft. Use a double boiler if you prefer. Otherwise stir over a low heat to prevent sticking.

O Add sugar and vanilla and stir until the mixture leaves the sides of the pan. Turn out onto a plate. Chill.

O Divide into pieces about the size of a small egg and roll on a floured board.

O Dip the croquettes in egg and breadcrumbs and deep fry in the vegetable oil at 170°C/325°F until golden brown.

O To make the peach sauce, sieve or blend the fruit.

O Mix the arrowroot with a little cold water and stir into the fruit mixture.

O Heat over a low heat until thickened and serve with the croquettes.

Mango and Kiwi Hedgehogs

o o o

SERVES 4

2 ripe mangoes
2 ripe kiwi fruits

425g/15oz canned or
    home-made creamy
    rice pudding

RIGHT AND BELOW
**Mango and Kiwi
Hedgehogs**

○ Cut the mangoes in half. Remove the stones. Run a small, sharp knife in straight lines down each half, scoring the fruit without cutting the skin.

○ Turn the halved, marked fruit inside out carefully.

○ Peel the kiwi fruits and slice. Arrange the kiwi slices in between the mango cubes.

○ Divide the rice in 4 portions on serving plates and top with the mango hedgehogs.

Milk Pudding

o o o

*T*his baked milk pudding is made with ground rice.

SERVES 3–4

600ml/1pt milk
50g/2oz ground rice
25g/1oz sugar
¼ tsp cinnamon

25g/1oz butter
oven temperature
    180°C/350°F/Gas 4

○ Heat the milk in a saucepan without boiling.

○ Butter an ovenproof dish which may have fruit or jam in the bottom or not, as liked.

○ Sprinkle the ground rice into the milk and continue stirring until the mixture comes to the boil and thickens. Remove from the heat.

○ Stir in the sugar and turn into the ovenproof dish, sprinkle with cinnamon and dot with butter. Bake for 25 minutes.

Pineapple Rice Pudding

○ ○ ○

SERVES 4

25g/1oz butter
50g/2oz short-grain
    rice
300ml/½pt evaporated
    milk
300ml/½pt water
25g/1oz sugar

2.5ml/½ tsp ground
    nutmeg
30ml/2 tbsp soft brown
    sugar
4 slices canned
    pineapple, drained
4 glacé cherries

○ Butter an ovenproof pie dish well.

○ Wash the rice several times in a sieve with running
cold water. Drain.

○ Pour the evaporated milk and water into the pie dish
and sprinkle the rice on top. Add the sugar and stir well.
If time allows leave to stand in the refrigerator for
1–2 hours as this improves the pudding.

○ Sprinkle with nutmeg and add a few small pieces of
butter to the surface.

○ Cover, with loose foil to prevent a skin from forming
and bake in the oven at 150°C/300°F/Gas 2 for 30–40
minutes on a low shelf, then stir well to separate the
grains. Continue cooking for a further 1–1¼ hours.

○ Remove the foil after 1¼ hours and sprinkle with the
brown sugar and arrange the pineapple rings on top.
Return to the oven for a further 30–40 minutes.

○ Decorate with glacé cherries in the centre of each
pineapple ring.

Shortbread

o o o

MAKES 2 CAKES

175g/6oz plain flour
75g/3oz ground rice
225g/8oz butter
125g/4oz sugar

a pinch of salt

oven temperature
170°C/325°F/Gas 3

O Sieve the flour and ground rice into a bowl.

O Making sure the butter is fairly soft, place it in another bowl and add the sugar. Squeeze the sugar and butter together by hand so they mix well but it is not necessary to cream the mixture.

O Add the salt to the flour and then gradually work in the lump of butter and sugar until a smooth ball is formed.

O Turn out onto a floured surface which is a mixture of ground rice and flour. Knead until smooth. Roll out

2 balls, shape in a thistle or decorated mould and turn onto a baking sheet. If a shortbread mould is not available cook two cakes in 15cm/6in flan rings or sandwich pans. Mark the edges.

O Cook in the oven for 1 hour.

O Sprinkle with sugar when cooling.

O This mixture may be rolled out and cut into biscuit shapes which will only take 20 minutes to cook.

O Alternatively, to make a delicious fruit shortcake, roll the mixture into an oblong about 1cm/½in thick. Cut off one oblong 18cm/7in long x 7.5cm/3in wide. Use this oblong as a base and cut the one left over into triangles. Once the shortbread pieces have been cooked, spread thick cream on the base, cover it with fruit and decorate it with the wedge shapes. Any suitable fruit can be used for decoration.

Index

○ ○ ○